Twayne's United States Authors Series

EDITOR OF THIS VOLUME

Warren French

Indiana University

Frank O'Hara

TUSAS 347

FRANK O'HARA

By ALAN FELDMAN

Framingham State College

TWAYNE PUBLISHERS

A DIVISION OF G. K. HALL & CO., BOSTON

Library of Congress Cataloging in Publication Data

Feldman, Alan, 1945–
Frank O'Hara.

(Twayne's United States authors series; TUSAS 347)
Bibliography: pp. 165–68
Includes index.
1. O'Hara, Frank—Criticism and interpretation.
PS3529.H28Z68   811'.5'4   79–11100
ISBN 0-8057-7277-4

For my grandfather, Alexander Abrams
and in memory of my grandmother, Lillian Abrams

For my father, Barney Feldman
and in memory of my mother, Goldye Feldman

—my first teachers

Contents

About the Author

Alan Feldman teaches creative writing and American literature at Framingham (Mass.) State College. He received his A.B. and M.A. degrees at Columbia University (where he edited the *Columbia Review*) and his Ph.D. at S.U.N.Y. at Buffalo (1973). His collection of poems, *The Happy Genius*, won the Elliston Award for 1978, and his poems, stories and essays have appeared in a number of magazines including *The Atlantic Monthly, The New American Review, Columbia Forum, College English, Audit/Poetry, Sun, Teachers and Writers Magazine,* and *Panache*. His work was chosen for the Borestone Mountain Awards volume *Best Poems of 1975*, and his fiction appears in *My Name Aloud* and *A Cinch*. In 1977–78 he was the recipient of a National Endowment for the Humanities fellowship.

Preface

This book about the poems of Frank O'Hara departs from the chronological organization most frequently used in presenting an overview of an author's work. The volumes O'Hara published during his lifetime have since been subsumed into the much more extensive collection of his work compiled by Donald Allen partly from unpublished manuscripts discovered in O'Hara's apartment at the time of his death in 1966. In 1971 Allen published *The Collected Poems* (five hundred and ten poems) and in 1977 supplemented it with two further volumes: *Early Writings* (eighty-five poems) and *Poems Retrieved* (one hundred and fifty-two poems). It seems at present that we have nearly the complete poems of Frank O'Hara. The question that remains, however, is what to make of this prolific mass.

Rather than proceeding volume by volume according to the dates in which O'Hara's poems first appeared in print, Allen has rightly decided to collate published and unpublished poems and present them in the order in which they were written. *The Collected Poems* (and its two supplementary volumes) in this way becomes something of a continuous unrevised and unabridged poetic sequence. Without the convenience of the original volumes to serve as milestones in the poet's career, a critic is faced with the alternatives of either providing his own chronological divisions or else finding some other method of dividing this large work into manageable parts. Since, in my view, O'Hara's development as a poet is overshadowed by the consistency of his vision and the innovative qualities displayed by his poetry throughout, I have organized my book according to the basic questions that can be asked of O'Hara's work as a whole: What is the language like? How (if at all) are the poems given coherence? What is the poet's overall subject and theme? What aesthetic goal is he trying to achieve? Does he have anything to say of a moral nature about his (and our) experience?

The chapters on O'Hara's language and structure are meant to prepare the ground for the discussions of theme, intention, and moral significance that follow. Where development within O'Hara's work has appeared significant to me, I have noted it; otherwise, my main concern is to describe the poems and comment upon them.

This study also seeks, however, to cull a selection of O'Hara's work out of the overall mass in order to bring into clearer focus O'Hara's most significant quality—a blend of personal intensity and comic detachment, a detachment which (and this only seems to be a paradox) results in an uncompromising authenticity of feeling. To base a survey of a poet's work on poems that illustrate a particular quality is, I think, justifiable when, as in O'Hara's case, there is as yet no canon to fall back on. But, more to the point, if I choose to emphasize what I consider to be O'Hara's unique strengths, and only briefly note his failings, it is because I am convinced that O'Hara is a far better poet than general critical opinion has yet recognized. I hope to correct an impression of him that is still widespread: that he is a writer who, because he is a homosexual, because he believes in art for art's sake, and because he is playful, fails to address the important concerns of ordinary life. On the contrary, O'Hara is one of the preeminent poets of everyday experience. His poetry illustrates the way in which art—while not ignoring the pain of existence—affirms life for it own sake. Not only because of his complex vision of affirmation, but also because of his innovative methods, O'Hara is one of the outstanding poets of the postwar era in America.

I am grateful to the National Endowment for the Humanities for awarding me a Fellowship in Residence during the 1977-78 academic year so that I could write a final version of this study. Helen Vendler, leader of the N.E.H. seminar at Boston University, read parts of the manuscript and offered advice and encouragement, as did my fellow seminar members, especially Paul Gaston (Southern Illinois University), T. Hunter Wilson (Marlborough College), and Pat Keene (Loyola University). I owe much to my friend and advisor Carl Dennis at the State University of New York at Buffalo for his patience and support when I was working on an earlier draft of this book. At that time, Kenneth Koch was also instrumental in helping me to get started; my debt to him, however, is even deeper and goes back further. I wrote a paper about O'Hara's humor in one of Koch's classes at Columbia College in 1964. Koch, O'Hara's close friend, was enthusiastic, but commented: "I think you could and should go further." I hope that, after all these years, I have.

Frank O'Hara's sister Maureen Granville-Smith, his friend Joseph LeSueur, and his Museum of Modern Art colleague Waldo Rasmussen, granted interviews and aided me greatly in piecing together my own vision of what O'Hara's life and personality were like. I had a helpful conversation, as well, with the poet Peter Schjeldahl who is now at work on O'Hara's biography. Alex Smith, the author of the first complete bibliography for O'Hara, kindly provided me with many articles I had not yet seen, and Ron Padgett saw to it that I received a copy of *The Selected Plays* before publication. I would also like to thank Stuart Byron and Bruce Boone for supplying me with copies of their important, but still difficult to obtain essays on O'Hara as a homosexual poet. My sister Judith Fetters helped edit part of the manuscript and offered some important suggestions. Laurel Bisson took charge of the overall editing and re-typing of the manuscript, but went much farther, pondering with me over details of interpretation. Her careful attention—both to my text and O'Hara's—improved the style and content of the manuscript throughout.

Throughout this book, numbers in parentheses refer to *The Collected Poems of Frank O'Hara*, edited by Donald Allen (New York, 1971), except when precceded by one of the following abbreviations:

AC   *Art Chronicles, 1954–1966* (New York, 1975)

EW   *Early Writing*, edited by Donald Allen (Bolinas, Cal., 1977)

HF   *Homage to Frank O'Hara*, edited by Bill Berkson and Joe LeSueur (Bolinas, Cal., 1978)

PR   *Poems Retrieved*, edited by Donald Allen (Bolinas, Cal., 1977)

SP   *The Selected Plays of Frank O'Hara,* edited by Ron Padgett (New York, 1978)

SS   *Standing Still and Walking in New York,* edited by Donald Allen (Bolinas, Cal., 1975).

ALAN FELDMAN

Framingham State College, Massachusetts

Acknowledgments

For permission to quote passages from published material, grateful acknowledgment is due:

Alfred A. Knopf, Inc., for permission to quote from *The Collected Poems of Frank O'Hara*, edited by Donald Allen. Copyright 1971 by Maureen Granville-Smith, Administratrix of the Estate of Frank O'Hara.

George Braziller, Inc., for permission to quote from *Art Chronicles, 1954–1966*. Copyright 1975 by Maureen Granville-Smith, Administratrix of the Estate of Frank O'Hara.

Full Court Press, Inc., for permission to quote from *The Selected Plays of Frank O'Hara*, edited by Ron Padgett, Joan Simon, and Anne Waldman. Copyright 1978 by Maureen Granville-Smith, Administratrix of the Estate of Frank O'Hara.

Donald Allen and Grey Fox Press, for permission to quote from *Standing Still and Walking in New York* by Frank O'Hara. Copyright 1975 by Maureen Granville-Smith, Administratrix of the Estate of Frank O'Hara. For permission to quote from *Poems Retrieved* by Frank O'Hara. Copyright 1977 by Maureen Granville-Smith, Administratrix of the Estate of Frank O'Hara. For permission to quote from *Early Writing* by Frank O'Hara. Copyright by Maureen Granville-Smith, Administratrix of the Estate of Frank O'Hara.

Maureen Granville-Smith for gracious permission to quote from "The 4th of July" by Frank O'Hara. Copyright 1979 by Maureen Granville-Smith, Administratrix of the Estate of Frank O'Hara.

The World Publishing Company for permission to quote from George Reavy's translation of Vladimir Mayakovsky's "An Ex-

Chronology

1926   Francis Russell O'Hara born in Baltimore on June 27, first child of Russell and Katherine (Broderick) O'Hara.

1927   Family moved to Grafton, Massachusetts.

1933–   Attended parochial schools in Worcester. Studied piano
1944   privately and then at New England Conservatory.

1944–   Served as sonarman third class on the destroyer U.S.S.
1946   Nicholas.

1946–   Attended Harvard College, majoring in music and then
1950   in English literature; A.B., 1950.

1950–   Graduate work at the University of Michigan. M.A. in
1951   comparative literature in 1951. Won major Hopwood Award for poetry. Moved to New York and worked at the Museum of Modern Art's information desk.

1952   *A City Winter and Other Poems.*

1953–   Editorial associate of *Art News*, writing reviews and
1955   occasional articles.

1955   Rejoined the Museum of Modern Art as a special assistant to Porter McCray, Director of the International Program, and assisted in preparing travelling exhibitions.

1956   Ford Foundation Fellowship to the Poets' Theatre, Cambridge, Mass., as playwright-in-residence, January to June.

1957   *Meditations in An Emergency.*

1958   *Stones*, with Larry Rivers.

1959   *Jackson Pollock.*

1960   O'Hara's work comprised the second largest selection in Donald Allen's *The New American Poetry, 1945–60. Odes* published, with serigraphs by Mike Goldberg. *The New Spanish Painting and Sculpture*, catalog for the Museum of Modern Art. *Awake in Spain* produced by The Living Theater. Appointed Assistant Curator of Painting and Sculpture Exhibitions, and travelled to Spain and Paris for the Museum.

1963 Taught poetry workshop at the New School for Social Research. Travelled to fourteen European cities to arrange exhibitions.

1964 *Lunch Poems*. Issue of *Audit/Poetry* devoted to his work. *The General Returns From One Place To Another* produced at the Writer's Stage Theatre.

1965 *Love Poems (Tentative Title)*. *Robert Motherwell*, catalog for the Museum of Modern Art. Appointed Associate Curator. Featured in the National Educational Television *USA: Poetry Series*.

1966 *David Smith* and *Nakian*, catalogs published by the Museum of Modern Art. Died July 25, 1966 after being hit by a dune buggy on Fire Island. Buried at Springs Cemetery, East Hampton.

1971 *The Collected Poems of Frank O'Hara*, edited by Donald Allen, received National Book Award.

1977 *Early Writing* and *Poems Retrieved*, also edited by Donald Allen.

1978 *Selected Plays*.

In an age in which disbelief is so profoundly prevalent or, if not disbelief, indifference to questions of belief, poetry and painting and the arts in general, are, in their measure, a compensation for what has been lost. Men feel that imagination is the next greatest power to faith: the reigning prince: consequently their interest in the imagination and its work is to be regarded not as a phase of humanism but as a vital self assertion in a world in which nothing but the self remains, if that remains.

—Wallace Stevens, *The Necessary Angel*

CHAPTER 1

Introduction: The Poet in New York

WHEN Wallace Stevens delivered his talk on "The Relation-ship Between Poetry and Painting" at the Museum of Modern Art in 1951, he might well have been prophesying the arrival of Frank O'Hara. Both as a poet and eventually as a cu-rator at the Museum of Modern Art, O'Hara was to devote him-self totally to the cause of art. For O'Hara the task of the artist was not to try to be a moral force or to influence society but to rescue something of the ephemeral and personal, to transform the energy of his own life into the enduring energy of art.

Yet Stevens's fascinating qualification about "a world in which nothing but the self remains, *if that remains*" applies particular-ly to O'Hara. For him, the task of self-assertion through artistic creativity was complicated by a view of the self as being almost entirely subject to its own fleeting moods and feelings. Tran-sience—both of the world and of the self—is O'Hara's overall theme. But his work is not cynical or nihilistic. His rejection of any sort of ideology—his denial even of a stable personal identity—leads him ultimately to an affirmation of life for its own sake.

To understand this fully we will have to rely on the poems themselves. First though, we will need to know something about O'Hara's career, particularly his life in New York and his con-nection with the art world. We will also want to know some-thing more about his vision of the world and the artist's role in it.

I Early Life

Frank O'Hara rarely wrote about his childhood in rural Graf-ton, Massachusetts; his preference for urban life was absolute: "I can't even enjoy a blade of grass," he once wrote, "unless I know there's a subway handy, or a record store or some other sign that people do not totally *regret* life" (197). The fragmen-

19

tary references to his early years that do occur in his poems, especially in his "Ode to Michael Goldberg ('s Birth and Other Births)," tell us something about why his rural childhood lacked meaning for him:

> Up on the mountainous hill
> behind the confusing house
> where I lived, I went each
> day after school and some nights
> with my various dogs . . .
>   . . . there,
>
> the wind sounded exactly like
> Stravinsky
>   I first recognized art
> as wildness, and it seemed right,
>   I mean rite, to me   (292)

Dogs, horses, people of this farm community appear as momentary curiosities in O'Hara's memory, but the true life of the poet could never be nourished here. It was urban art and culture, music and movies at first, and later poetry and visual arts, dance, and urban architecture that were to make up his true world.

The poet's family was conventionally middle class. His father, Russell J. O'Hara, was a native of Grafton, a farm town southeast of Worcester; his mother, Katherine Broderick, from Worcester, enrolled in a business college where Russell, a graduate of Holy Cross, was teaching. After their marriage, the couple moved to Baltimore for a year where Russell managed a haberdashery. Shortly after their first child Francis Russell O'Hara was born, on June 27, 1926, they returned to Grafton where Russell took over the management of the family's three farms and a dealership for farm machinery. The family lived in Grafton throughout Frank's childhood, and he, his younger brother Phillip (J. Phillip O'Hara, the Chicago publisher), and his sister Maureen (now Maureen Granville-Smith of Rowaton, Connecticut) all grew up there.

The O'Haras, especially the father, were strict Catholics, and Frank was sent to parochial schools in Worcester. In "Autobiographical Fragments" O'Hara recalls his early rejection of Catholicism:

I had rather summarily deduced that my whole family were liars and, since our "community" consisted of a by and large very mixed national descendency it couldn't be that they were Irish liars, they must be Catholic liars. . . . I blamed almost everything on the Catholic Church, which they all talked about in the most revoltingly smarmy way (a priest once later said, trying to win me over, that I had been overparochialized!). I left the Truth to Music. (SS, 30)

Though he says nothing more explicit about it, it could well be that O'Hara's early recognition of his own homosexuality led to an early and complete break with the Catholic Church (in whose eyes he was damned) and to a rejection of all religious belief. This, in turn, strengthened the independence of spirit needed to do original and creative work. Art—particularly music at this point—had to be the "compensation" Stevens spoke of, the chief source of significance in the absence of belief.

O'Hara began to study piano at the age of seven, and, by the time he was seventeen, he had made up his mind to be a great pianist and composer like Rachmaninoff. In 1944, on graduation from St. John's High School in Worcester, O'Hara enlisted in the Navy. After receiving basic training in Norfolk, Virginia, he was stationed in San Francisco for a period (where he continued studying piano and went to concerts) and walked his beat in the bar and nightclub area as a member of the Shore Patrol. He then served on the destroyer U.S.S. Nicholas in the South Pacific. Though he was not engaged in actual combat, he was close to the scene of it.

O'Hara wrote about these years in detail only once, in an early prose piece called "Lament and Chastisement: A Travelogue of War and Personality." Here, recalling his own growing recognition of the barbarity of killing, O'Hara reports his own inner disassociation from any feeling of victory or patriotic pride. Though such disillusionment was not unusual, what sets O'Hara apart was his affirmation of the primacy of art and the individual life over historical events:

At this time I reread *Ulysses*, needing to throw up my sensibility

and Joyce's art into the face of my surroundings; I found that Joyce
was more than a match, I was reassured that what was important
to me would always be important to me; deprived of music I wrote
pieces which turned out to sound something like early Bartok, and
I wrote awful poetry compounded of Donne, Whitman and Cum-
mings, which I later destroyed. I found that I myself was my life:
it had not occurred to me before; now I knew that the counters
with which I dealt with my life were as valid in unsympathetic
surroundings as they had been in sympathetic ones; for art is never
a retreat; the person who cannot face himself enough to face the
world on certain given terms may find that other terms are more
suitable to his psyche: this is a matter of self-knowledge, not
cowardice. . . . (*EW*, 122–23)

On leaving the Navy in 1946, O'Hara entered Harvard, majoring in music his first year, then switching to English literature.

At Harvard, O'Hara read widely, not only the classics of English
literature prescribed by his courses, but also French and German poetry and the works of then-little-known fiction writers
like Samuel Beckett, Jean Rhys, Flann O'Brien and Ronald Fir-
bank. Cambridge was full of young poets in those years who
would go on to be well known (Robert Bly, Robert Creeley,
Donald Hall, Adrienne Rich, Richard Wilbur) but O'Hara did
not know them very well, if at all. Though some of his early writings were published in the *Harvard Advocate*, his most important literary friendship at Harvard came about because of his
advanced knowledge of contemporary music. O'Hara's friend
and fellow poet, John Ashbery, recalls that they met only in their
senior year when, to his surprise, he overheard someone say at
a party in a voice and tone very much like his own: "Let's face
it, [Poulenc's] *Les Sécheresses* is greater than [Wagner's] *Tristan*."
Ashbery goes on to explain that in those "dull and snobbish"
days at Harvard nobody took Poulenc or most other modern
composers seriously, and that O'Hara's remark was deliberately
meant to be provocative: "Frank didn't really believe *Les
Sécheresses* was greater than *Tristan* . . . but at the same time
he felt . . . that art is already serious enough; there is no point in
making it seem even more serious by taking it too seriously" (*HF*, 20).

Looking back on himself and Frank O'Hara as they were at

Harvard, Ashbery recalls: "We were serious but we were also a little unintentionally funny in our aesthete's pose, a little pathetic. Nobody but ourselves and a handful of adepts knew or cared about our poetry, or seemed likely to in the future.... Later on, in the more encouraging climate of New York, we could begin to be ourselves, but much of the poetry we both wrote as undergraduates now seems marred by a certain nervous preciosity, in part a reaction to the cultivated blandness around us..." (*HF*, 21).

That O'Hara was already a dedicated and serious writer while still at Harvard is evident from the journal he kept in his senior year. O'Hara's journal shows his precocious range of reading, his intelligence, his ongoing debate about just how wicked it will be necessary for him to be, his humorous confrontation with what Camus called the main question of modern man ("I often wish I had the strength to commit suicide, but on the other hand, if I had, I probably wouldn't feel the need," *EW*, 100), but most of all his passionate, all-consuming desire to write: "... Simply to live does not justify existence," he declared with youthful fervor, "for life is a mere gesture on the surface of the earth, and death a return to that from which we had never been wholly separated; but oh to leave a trace, no matter how faint, of that brief gesture! For someone, some day, may find it beautiful!" (*EW*, 105).

On graduating from Harvard in 1950, O'Hara pursued his interest in literature by accepting a graduate fellowship in comparative literature at the University of Michigan. His objectives seem to have been to remove himself from the Boston area, to devote a year to writing poetry, and to compete in the University's prestigious Hopwood competition. A manuscript of his poems, "A Byzantine Place," and a verse play, *Try! Try!*, did indeed win him a major Hopwood Award, but the year in Michigan was a year of displacement and loneliness. In the autumn of 1951, after receiving his M.A., O'Hara joined Ashbery in New York, worked briefly as a secretary for the photographer and designer, Cecil Beaton, and then found a job in the bookstore at the Museum of Modern Art. New York, the museum, and friendships with New York artists and writers he had already begun to make—these were to be the mainstays of his existence for the remaining years of his short but productive life.

II *New York*

> *Poet of building-glass*
> *I see you walking you said with your tie*
> *flopped over your shoulder . . .*
>
> •   •   •   •
>
> *Curator of funny emotions to the mob,*
> *Trembling One, whenever possible. I see New York through*
> *your eyes . . .*
> *appreciated more and more*
> *a common ear*
> *for our deep gossip.*
> —Allen Ginsberg, "City Midnight Junk Strains"[1]

Before Frank O'Hara, the only important American poet ever to love an American city was Walt Whitman. Whitman most shows his love not during his bravado exclamations about Manhattan's grandeur, nor during his wide-sweeping panoramas of the street, but when he ingenuously confesses that he enjoys flattening his nose against the plate glass of a store window. O'Hara's poetry is full of just such minute but authentic gestures of love and perceptions of city pleasures. He was indeed, as Allen Ginsberg said of him in the elegy he wrote after the poet's death, "City Midnight Junk Strains," a "poet of building-glass." He is the first American writer to see the city not only as a lovable melting-pot or a den of sin, but as a work of art: "where does the evil of the year go/ when September takes New York/ and turns it into ozone stalagmites/ deposits of light" (340). O'Hara became America's most enthusiastic poet of city life. He also became a central figure in the New York art and literary world during one of its most creative periods.

New York in the late 1940's and early 1950's saw the birth of American Abstract Expressionism, the most influential and original movement in the history of American art. The "drip" paintings of Pollock (sometimes called "action paintings"), the colorful, rapidly brushed canvases of Willem de Kooning, the stark, gigantic, calligraphic black, white and gray paintings of Franz Kline, were among the works that influenced a whole generation of New York painters—a group that became known as the New York School. It was these painters who provided an audience for the young New York poets—Frank O'Hara, John Ashbery, Kenneth Koch among them—as part of an antiestablishment alliance, and the result was an unprecedented degree of artistic cross-fertilization, both through informal gatherings in favorite bars and through panel discussions at *The Club,* an organization founded by the Abstract Expressionists in the late 1940's. In this avant-garde art scene of the 1950's, O'Hara soon assumed a central position.

The story of O'Hara's years in New York must take into account his career at the Museum of Modern Art, his prolific writings for arts publications, his collaborations with artists, his writings for the stage, and, finally and most importantly, his own poetry.

Had he never written a single poem, O'Hara's extraordinarily productive and successful career at the Museum of Modern Art would have been sufficient testimony to his brilliance and energy. He began as a nonprofessional employee in 1951. But by 1955, when he was hired to serve as an administrative assistant to Porter McCray, director of the Museum's recently established International Program, he was already very much a part of the New York art world. Since 1953 he had been writing articles for *Art News* and had participated in numerous panels at *The Club.* Encouraged and taught by McCray, he was soon able to assume curatorial work.

O'Hara's first assignment of this kind was to work on an exhibition of Abstract Expressionist art entitled *The New American Painting,* the first museum exhibition devoted exclusively to this important movement to be shown both in the United States and abroad. Waldo Rasmussen, now Director of the International Program at the Museum, recalls that the exhibition might not have taken place at all if he and O'Hara had not drafted a memorandum declaring that though time was short they would be willing to work overtime to see that all the arrangements could be made: "Frank and I worked very closely on these things because we both believed in Abstract Expressionism and wanted to do something about it."[2] The exhibition, directed by Dorothy C. Miller, was shown simultaneously with an exhibition devoted exclusively to the paintings of Jackson Pollock. O'Hara was responsible for revising the Pollock exhibition for showing abroad and, in Rasmussen's view, "the exhibition

he selected was brilliant.... Frank's selection showed more of
the process of Pollock's art, providing a clearer image of his
early development and of those troubled last years from 1953 to
1955 when Pollock was trying out different styles.... An inveter-
ate defender of the difficult, he had a special predilection for
sensibilities which could be stubbornly independent" (*HF*, 88).

In the following nine years, O'Hara directed or codirected
nineteen exhibitions. Appointed Assistant Curator in 1960,
promoted to Associate Curator in 1965, he was due for promotion
to a full curatorship at the time of his death. Rapid as it was,
his advancement would probably have been faster had there
not been among some of his colleagues a suspicion of this gifted
amateur whose opinions were often more in the nature of
passionate advocacy than reserved professional judgment. However, in Rasmussen's view, O'Hara was able to use his position
at the Museum to advance the cause of artists he believed in
without succumbing to personal favoritism. His involvement
with many artists aided the Museum in exhibiting representative
works of some of the best recent American and European art. As
painter John Button put it: "Frank's civility and wildness as well
as his comprehensive knowledge of post-war art and artists were
indispensible.... I worked [at the Museum] much of the time
Frank did, and I could see that they had curators who were
good scholars, curators who could shake the hands of patrons,
and curators who could be snooty at parties. But they had no
one who was at home among the newly emerging artists and
was also 'presentable.' Frank needed a job. The Museum needed
Frank. So he entered the establishment art world and brought
to it his own non-establishment style" (*HF*, 42).

O'Hara's art criticism, which can now be found in the collections *Art Chronicles* and *Standing Still and Walking in New
York,* ranges from the more formal critical introductions he
wrote for the Museum's catalogs to improvisational, personal
narratives of his wanderings through museums and galleries and
artists' studios, the art chronicles. His theoretical formulations on
art are not systematic, nor was he very often an objective critic
who assessed strengths and weaknesses. His virtue as a critic
was his ability to describe a work of art as an experience. In
Jackson Pollock (1959), an early book-length study, O'Hara
gives Pollock's intense, ultimately abstract "drip" paintings con-

creteness by linking them with images in his own imagination: "*Eyes in the Heat II*," he says of one of Pollock's canvases, "has a blazing, acrid, dangerous glamor of a legendary kind, not unlike those volcanoes which are said to lure the native to the lip of the crater and, by the beauty of their writhings and the strength of their fumes, cause him to fall in" (*AC*, 29–30). The core of O'Hara's criticism is in the meaning of art *to him*. Pollock's heroic paintings gave O'Hara confidence in the victory of art and of "seeing" over darkness and death. As he says in his lovely poem on one of Pollock's paintings, his "Digression on *Number 1, 1948*," which he includes in his study:

> Stars are out and there is sea
> enough beneath the glistening earth
> to bear me toward the future
> which is not so dark. I see.   (260)

Indeed, his critical writings are at their best when he is reenacting the process of seeing. His humorous and perceptive description of the Guggenheim Museum at the beginning of "Art Chronicle I" serves as one example:

It's wonderful looking from the outside, and when you enter the flat exhibition space on the ground floor the effect of the works near at hand, the ramps and over them glimpses of canvases and then the dome, is urbane and charming, like the home of a cultivated and mildly eccentric person. The elevator is a good idea too. . . . It takes off the curse of most elevators, which is that when you go up in an elevator in the daytime you are usually going to some unpleasant experience like work or a job interview, but here you are going up for pleasure. . . . Anyhow, I like the whole experience, the "bins" where you come around a semi-wall and find a masterpiece has had its back to you, the relation between seeing a painting or a sequence of them from across the ramp and then having a decent interval of time and distraction intervene before the close scrutiny: in general my idea is that this may not be (as what is) the ideal museum, but in this instance Frank Lloyd Wright was right in the lovable way that Sophie Tucker was to get her gold tea set, which she described as, "It's way out on the nut for service, but it was my dream!"   (*AC*, 1–2)

Without confronting the issue argumentatively, O'Hara suggests through his witty comparisons that the Museum's strong point is the impression it gives of exciting and eccentric hospitality. (The museum is like a host and "a masterpiece," like a famous guest, "has had its back to you.") Surely at O'Hara's irreverent but charming comparison of Wright's museum to Sophie Tucker's gold tea service, the critical controversy ought to have subsided into friendly laughter.

Of the various collaborations Frank O'Hara did with painters, preeminence must be given to *Stones*, the series of lithographs O'Hara did with Larry Rivers between 1957 and 1960. Such works, as Marjorie Perloff has pointed out, constitute a true hybrid genre.[3] O'Hara and Rivers worked together directly on the stones from which the prints would be made (O'Hara having learned to put his text in, himself, in mirror-writing). In *Stones* both artist and poet play an equal role—the artist is not an illustrator, the poet is not a caption-writer or commentator. For example, in describing the creation of the lithograph known as "Love," Rivers stresses the process of dual improvisation that went into making it: "We decided to do a LOVE stone. I distributed male and female over the surface with a few genitalia for the sex of it. He [O'Hara] wrote in between and on the drawing and never even mentioned man or woman or bodies or sex."[4]

On the whole, *Stones* records the process of interaction between O'Hara and Rivers, and thus represents an artistic integration of considerable importance. Of all the artists he knew, O'Hara seems to have been closest in temperament to Larry Rivers, of whom he once wrote: "Rivers' . . . work is very much a diary of his experience. He is inspired directly by visual stimulation and his work is ambitious to save these experiences. Where much of the art of our time has been involved with direct conceptual or ethical considerations, Rivers has chosen to mirror his preoccupations and enthusiasms in an unprogrammatic way" (SS, 171).

O'Hara met Rivers in 1950 and they remained close friends to the end of O'Hara's life. He was Rivers's model many times, appearing almost as frequently in his work as Rivers's now-famous mother-in-law, Berdie (Mrs. Bertha Berger). O'Hara appears in some of Rivers's best known paintings, including *The*

Studio (1956) and *The Athlete's Dream* (1956), and in a nude study, *O'Hara* (1954).

Cooperation and mutual support were important to their friendship. Rivers recollects first asking O'Hara to model in the autumn of 1952: "That was after I'd slit my wrists over something. I phoned Frank, who happened to be in, and he came over and bandaged me up. . . . There was always a dialogue going on during our working sessions. He gave me feedback and made me feel what I was doing mattered, and after a while I found I needed him for my work" (*HF*, 57). The relationship, both sexual and creative, encouraged O'Hara's work as well. "As early as 1952," O'Hara recalls, "Larry did a set for a play of mine, *Try! Try!* At the first run-through I realized it was all wrong and withdrew it. He, however, insisted that if he had done the work for the set I should be willing to rewrite to my own satisfaction, and so I rewrote the play for [the actors] and Larry's set. . . . Few people are so generous toward the work of others" (*SS*, 172).

O'Hara also did a series of poem-paintings with the artist Norman Bluhm in 1960—rapid brush designs with brief poems or phrases by O'Hara (now in the New York University Art collection). Unlike the *Stones* series, these have the advantage of having been done frontwards so that O'Hara's rapid, flowing handwriting matches the action of the design, and enhances it. Also, since Bluhm's designs are more abstract, O'Hara's texts can interact more freely with them; his phrases or poems become tiny acts of interpretation, offering concrete and sometimes surprising responses in the same way that his criticism helps us to discover an emotional dimension in Pollock's grand and otherwise impersonal paintings. Though O'Hara's texts for these works are not his best poetry, both *Stones* and the "poem-paintings" do offer the record of a lively, personal dialogue between two artists working in different media.

III *Playwright*

As we might suspect when he tells us that he rewrote *Try! Try!* "for" Larry Rivers's sets, O'Hara regarded the many plays that he wrote as collaborative works of art also. The receptivity of New York groups like the Artist's Theater and the Living

Theater encouraged poets and artists to team up in creating innovative theater pieces. O'Hara wrote or collaborated on at least twenty-six plays or fragments of plays in his career. Three are known to have been lost and twenty-three can be found in the *Selected Plays*. Like the poem-paintings, the plays attempt and achieve less than O'Hara's poems but are valuable as records of cultural happenings.

Awake in Spain (written in 1953 and produced by the Living Theater in 1960) is perhaps the most remarkable of them. The play is written for eighty-four characters and groups of characters, most of whom have no more than one line to speak. These include: Generalissimo Franco, Joan Crawford, Larry Rivers, A Statue of Delores Del Rio, Sodom, a 1936 Chevrolet, William Blake, Spanish Refugees, the Empire State Building, Benjamin Franklin, a Village Flapper, and various members of the Spanish royal family. O'Hara's wacky, surreal set descriptions might well have provided Larry Rivers with a considerable challenge:

Act I: A sky filthy with bangles, but soft, somehow, and pensive. There is a verdant meadow upside down in the center of the stage and many unhabituated animals stroll about, as if at a fashion show. A large pair of lips, greasily rouged, smile from the rear wall. (*SP*, 96)

The play's main action is the reestablishment of the Spanish monarchy by the crown prince (whose name is Frank). At the end of the play, however, the king's younger son (who was kept in school in Switzerland even though he was forty years old) has declared war on his brother. But this "plot" is buried in a bewildering array of scene changes and disconnected remarks. And as the play goes on the set descriptions get even stranger and seemingly more difficult to execute. For example, Part I, Act II takes place in the trough of a wave somewhere off the Iberian Peninsula; Act III calls for a "brilliant ballroom hung with wigs"; Act V: "Tears flowing down the walls, and a marimba in the center of the stage with several people napping on it"; and Part III, Act I requires "fifty-three old caretakers . . . stuffed into a blue bathing suit." One of the only threads of continuity is the repeated stage direction: "A parade goes by, inescapably alert." Indeed, with its sequence of characters in various costumes (most of whom are only seen once) and its rapid changing of sets, the play might have produced something of the effect of an indoor parade with strange floats. In fact, however, the difficulties of a production of this type proved insuperable. The actors sat at a table, while a narrator read the stage directions and identified the many characters.

One of the themes of *Awake in Spain* seems to be change and discontinuity (it concludes with Thomas Hardy saying "O dynasties, incessantly tumbling!"). The rewritten version of *Try! Try!* (1953) deals with this theme more explicitly and on a more domestic scale. John and Violet have been living together while Jack, Violet's husband, has been away fighting in the war. As their names suggest, the two men are virtually interchangeable—at least they are in Violet's life. When Jack comes home, John refuses to apologize to him or to give Violet up:

> I suppose I'm the snake-in-the-grass but
> I can't say I'm sorry. Someone has to smile
> at her as she comes back from the bathroom.
> Do you think everything can stay the same,
> like a photograph? What for? (*SP*, 48)

What distinguishes *Try! Try!* from an ordinary love-triangle story is the care with which the characters avoid making their feelings explicit, or the witty and sometimes enigmatical and excessive metaphors they use if they do talk about them. When Jack finds that he has been displaced by John and leaves, Violet launches into a kind of aria about all the things she would like to turn into, and about the miraculous powers she'd like to have:

> If I were the sphinx I could lie
> in the sun and stare at myself
> with pure white eyes. When I smiled
> airplanes would go off their courses.
> I'd hold down the dark and say
> sweet nothings to the palms. (*SP*, 49)

In reply to her speech, John says: "Honey, I designed that costume for you./ You always look like that to me./ That's why I'm so mean." Indeed, the language of the play is itself a costume, and the play a soap opera dressed up in surreal verse.

O'Hara's poetry contributed an important element to the overall effect of both *Try! Try!* and *Awake in Spain*. In his last produced play, *The General Returns From One Place To Another*, O'Hara becomes more of a satirist than a poet-play-wright. The General, like General MacArthur, has an obsession with returning to places. Sensing that life is transition, the General tries to mask that fact by wandering around only in places he is convinced he has been to before. He has become known as something of a pest in the South Pacific, and the natives do not always welcome him with enthusiasm. But, as the General explains it, "The point is to come back, not to be recognized. Art's long, and conquered people are short. That's why they don't recognize me ..." (*SP*, 195). The General, who expresses himself in an odd blend of press conference language and poetic clichés, eventually dies in a field of flowers, possibly on the brink of discovering love and art. "God! He never did that before," one of his aides says, and the other responds: "Well of course not, you dope. You only *can* do that once!" (*SP*, 216–17). After a life of comical repetition and rigidity the General's death forces a new experience on him at last. The General begins the play "almost nude but wearing galoshes and a toupee" (*SP*, 188), and adds one article of clothing to himself each scene, until he dies, presumably, in full uniform, "returning" to his proper appearance as a man of authority, yet one without the power to grow and change.

IV *The Last Days*

O'Hara's many activities in New York—his career at the Museum, his writings on art, his collaborations with artists, his plays—did not seem to interfere with his poetry. On the contrary, his friend and fellow poet James Schuyler believes that O'Hara's absorption in the cultural milieu of New York, particularly the art world, distracted him from the pressure of having to be constantly obsessed with his own creativity, and thus may have helped his poetry: "I think you are hampered," Schuyler writes in a letter to John Ashbery, "by a feeling of disapproval, or irritation (also felt by others ...) of Frank's exaltation of the New York painters as the climax of human creativity, as something more important than his own work and talent. Perhaps the kindest (and it may even be true) way of seeing it would be along the lines of what Pasternak says about life creating incidents to divert our attention from it so that it can get on with the work it can only accomplish unobserved" (ix).

O'Hara wrote prolifically, and did produce a good deal of his poetry "unobserved." At the time of his death in 1966 he had published only a fraction of the more than seven hundred poems that we now have, and much of what was published appeared in small-press limited editions, or in little magazines. His first books were *A City Winter and Other Poems* (1952) with drawings by Larry Rivers and *Oranges* (1953) with a hand painted cover by Grace Hartigan, both published by John Myers, owner of the Tibor de Nagy Gallery. In 1957, he published his first book of poems with a commercial press, *Meditations in An Emergency,* though even this had an initial press run of only one thousand copies. He first came to national attention through the generous selection of his work in Donald Allen's groundbreaking anthology *The New American Poetry 1945–1960* (New York: Grove Press, 1960). Allen not only reprinted some of O'Hara's best poems from *Meditations,* but also included a number of important poems previously unpublished anywhere. Allen's anthology was regarded as the best source of information about new poetry in America at that time, and O'Hara's work became widely known through the impressive sample Allen selected. *Odes* (1960), published in an extremely large format with five serigraphs by Mike Goldberg, contained some of O'Hara's best poetry but was bought, presumably, mostly by art collectors. (The text alone was reprinted by The Poets Press in New York in 1969). O'Hara's long poem, *Second Avenue* (1953), was published in pamphlet form in 1960. In 1964 the prestigious Pocket Poets series of City Lights Books (edited by Lawrence Ferlinghetti) published a collection of O'Hara's poems, *Lunch Poems,* written between 1954 and 1964. That year, another book-length selection of O'Hara's poems was published as an issue of *Audit/Poetry* (Buffalo, New York) and a selection of his love poems, *Love Poems (Tentative Title),* was published by John Myers of Tibor de Nagy in 1965. These volumes contained, altogether, no more than half of O'Hara's poetry, and of these volumes only *Lunch*

Poems was readily available to book buyers outside New York at
the time of O'Hara's death.

Only in the final two years of his life—possibly because of
increased responsibilities at the Museum, or because of some personal crisis—did his creativity as a poet seem to stop. Until 1964
he had averaged fifty poems a year, often writing many more,
but between May 1964 and his death at the age of forty on July
25, 1966 he wrote no more than five poems. Among his effects
after his death his friends found a composition notebook with
his name on it, with an entry dated 4/7/66:

> *Oedipus Rex*
>   He falls; but even in falling
> he is higher than those who
> fly into the ordinary sun.   (*HF*, 146)

The rest of the pages were blank.

O'Hara was struck by a beach buggy on Fire Island shortly
before dawn on Sunday morning, July 24, when he and a group
of friends were waiting beside their disabled beach taxi for
another to pick them up. O'Hara's friend, J. J. Mitchell, who
was present at the time, recalls that the impatient passengers,
returning from a party, were milling about: "It was probably
about 3 a.m. The rest is a hazy nightmare. A beach buggy
approached, traveling toward us in the ruts created in the
sand by the previous taxis. (Near the water where the wet
packed sand afforded an accelerated speed.) For reasons that
remain fuzzy to this day (the 21-year-old driver—with girl-
friend—said he was blinded by our headlights), the beach buggy
failed to slow down, passed perilously close to our taxi, causing
at least nine of us to jump hastily aside, and collided head-on
with Frank, who had strayed momentarily away from me and
the group" (*HF*, 144–45). O'Hara died at 8:50 the next evening
in Bayview Hospital, Mastic Beach, Long Island, and was
buried at Springs Cemetery, near East Hampton.

Certain poets are "meant" to die young; O'Hara had always
assumed he was one of them, as did some of his friends: "I
had always thought [Frank] would be the first to die among my
small happy group," Larry Rivers said at the funeral. "But I
day-dreamed a romantic death brought about by too much

whiskey, by smoking three packs of Camels a day, by too much sex, by unhappy love affairs, by writing too many emotional poems, too many music and dance concerts, just too much living..." (*HF*, 138). Rivers praised O'Hara's emotional responsiveness and energy. In their memoirs, O'Hara's friends also like to recall his interest in and encouragement of other poets and artists, his inner self-pride and self-confidence and his charming modesty. He seems to have had a limitless capacity to be a close friend to many people, and to have always been willing to make room in his life for someone new. One of the younger poets O'Hara encouraged, Bill Berkson, has edited a volume of memoirs of O'Hara written by some of the many people who knew him. The epigraph to Berkson and LeSueur's introduction to the *Homage to Frank O'Hara* (1978) is taken from Pasternak's *Dr. Zhivago*: "You in others—that is your soul." And indeed, the story of O'Hara's life is also the history of O'Hara-in-others, of his many relationships with the people of the New York art and literary world.

V *The Coherent Instant: O'Hara's Vision*

O'Hara refers to art as the highest source of meaning, yet at the same time he feels that the artist need not look for meaning or attempt to confer it. To try to resolve this paradox we can consider for a moment O'Hara's only extended piece of literary criticism, his essay on Pasternak's *Dr. Zhivago*, which provides us with an account of O'Hara's own beliefs about art and its relationship to human life.

In "About Zhivago and His Poems" (1959), O'Hara tells us that Zhivago exemplifies Pasternak's belief that the poet "is not a living personality absorbed in the study of moral knowledge, but a visual-biographical 'emblem,' demanding a background to make his contours visible." As such, his writings, though centered on his own responses, articulate both himself and his world. When Zhivago is mourning for Lara he "saves his sanity" by writing. O'Hara concludes that in his poems Zhivago achieves his "triumph over the terrible vicissitudes of love and circumstance ... the 'active manifestation' of himself—his soul, his immortality, his life in others" (505). Contrasting Zhivago with the "active" Red Army Commissar, Strelnikov, O'Hara articulates

his belief in the supremacy of art over history, and of the artist
over the man of action: "Strelnikov... is rendered passive by
his blind espousal of principles whose needful occasion has
passed; Zhivago, passively withdrawn from action which his
conscience cannot sanction, finds the art for which an occasion
will continue to exist" (507). Aware that one cannot live by
"principle," but only within the flow of "conscience," the artist
must "perceive and articulate," looking for permanent meaning in
self-expression, which is also the expression of others through
him.

In linking Pasternak to O'Hara, however, we must take into
account the vast difference in their historical circumstances.
Pasternak's poems (like those of his main character Dr. Zhivago)
are moments of personal illumination about love and history
from the midst of an era of terrible suffering; O'Hara's poems
illuminate the life of a man free to enjoy the pleasures and
excitements of a great city in relatively peaceful times. But the
common element is the belief in the primary importance of the
artist's role, apart from any ideology or set of moral principles.
The poet faces his life with "unrelenting honesty" and must
"perceive and articulate and, like Zhivago, choose love above all
else" (509). The absence of ideology ought not to be replaced
by nihilism or cynicism but must coexist with a love of man
and of life itself.

If an author's work can be said to have a point of origin, some
point at which he articulates his overall intention, then such a
moment can be found in the typescript of O'Hara's as yet unpublished novel, *The 4th of July*, when Bud, a young poet and
avatar of O'Hara, stands on the beach staring at the waves—
"infinitely numerous and energetic"—rushing towards him:

The sun and wind dried him, little grains of salt lay on his skin
and hair. He felt too good to lie down on the sand so went walking
along the beach, just ankle deep in the glassy water, feeling it
suck away at his feet and then flood back in, watching the patterns
disappear and change, like abstract and instantaneous photographs,
compositions of water and foam and sand, fleeting, but sharp and
definite for their instant of coherence. He was glad to be here to
see them, for they would never recur. And no one else would ever
see them.

Bud's gladness at being able to seize the fleeting compositions of water and sand in their "instant of coherence" is that in doing so he seizes an instant of coherence in his life and gives a moment of his own experience meaning. But coherence is fleeting. Whereas a man with another sort of temperament might prefer to think about the eternal quality of the sea, Bud's gladness is a response to the process of change and continual motion he observes. He is not carrying a camera; the patterns of the water are not there to be recorded. It is not the pattern itself that is beautiful but the experience of suddenly becoming aware of a pattern that is already pulling away towards its own dissolution.

From the very beginning of his career as a writer, O'Hara resolves to make the flow of his own life and feelings his subject, rather than any set of ideas or beliefs. In terms very much like that of his Zhivago essay, he asserts in his college journal his belief in the artist's need to love and create without recourse to ideology:

I feel steadily but there is no pattern, there can be no pattern, there is only being; you cannot sell yourself, you cannot stand that far apart from your self to dicker, if there is any integrity in you. There is only the giving of self and the having, the always being; you must *be* to always love and always create, the artist *is* and always loves and always creates and cannot help but love and create. . . . There is no need for a pattern if one lives, for in the realization of being one can cope with life as it comes with suffering but no bitterness. (*EW*, 110)

Part of O'Hara's uniqueness as a poet, and also his chief difficulty for readers, is his absence of pattern, or what Helen Vendler has called his "utter absence . . . of an intellectual syntax."[5] Indeed, O'Hara seems willing to brave experience without recourse to the safety of some sort of anchoring overall idea. No good O'Hara poem—indeed, no work of art—can be without some sort of form, but O'Hara seeks to create forms that are as close as possible to the "formlessness" of experience. These poems are not like photographs, they do not seek to impose a composition on the momentary, but they do try to record the instant at which experience is gathering itself into something that deserves the artist's attention, a confluence of feeling and perception that is suffused with a sense of its own passing away.

The city landscape, disconnected from the harmony and cyclical rhythms of nature, is thus O'Hara's proper milieu. The city bristles with particularity, and is full of signs and labels that announce the uniqueness and transience of each event. A truck in a stream of traffic has a sign on it to distinguish it from others; its meaning is derived from its uniqueness. It does not seem to belong to the eternity of nature and art, but only to the momentary and impermanent flow of commerce. But O'Hara's poetry, which is full of the names of particular restaurants and bars, which celebrates the particularity of billboards and the names of actual people (friends, celebrities, other artists) tries to render this texture of particularity and impermanence in a work of art that lifts it above its own impermanence. It does this by weaving the flow of city life together with the flow of feeling in the poet's life. At its best, such an amalgam has a firmness, just as Bud's gladness could be translated into art were he to write a poem. The particular patterns of places and people disappear, but the pattern of human feeling and response remains.

The experiences that provide the occasions for O'Hara's poems often involve other works of art. "Sometimes I think I'm 'in love' with painting" (329) he once wrote. Though painting was the preeminent art form for him, he might have said the same for music, dance, and film as well. In a city world of man-made experiences, art objects often provide the most intense stimuli.

Yet perhaps his most pervasive subject is his relationship to the city itself. Here too, as with works of art, it is O'Hara's emotional and imaginative journeying in the city that is the real subject; the city itself—the buildings, the incongruous names, the snippets of conversations with strangers, the offerings of trashy re-run movies—is used as an abundant source of images.

In "Rhapsody," for example, the city landscape is fragmented into a dreamlike montage. O'Hara describes walking down Madison Avenue, passing 515 (an entryway that always fascinated him), having just come from a favorite Elizabeth Taylor movie (*Rhapsody*, 1954). The city is not the subject, but rather his own movement of feeling within that complex setting:

> 515 Madison Avenue
> door to heaven? portal

> stopped realities and eternal licentiousness
> or at least the jungle of impossible eagerness
> your marble is bronze and your lianas elevator cables
> swinging from the myth of ascending
> I would join

The syntax here is not merely descriptive, but leaps to jungle images as the elevator cables become liana vines. Suddenly this familiar, mystifying "portal" of 515 Madison Avenue becomes a metaphor for the portal that leads to rhapsodic experience, and under the pressure of O'Hara's mood the city rearranges itself into an exotic landscape.

O'Hara's New York never ceases to be the real New York as well. But it can suddenly seem ablaze with a kind of high-altitude light, an image that is both ecstatically inspiring and familiar at the same time. Later, even a short conversation with a cab driver takes its place in the exalted flow of things.

At the conclusion of the poem, the subject is no longer even nominally Madison Avenue or New York, but death as a moment of rhapsodic enlightenment:

> I have always wanted to be near it
> though the day is long (and I don't mean Madison Avenue)
> lying in a hammock on St. Mark's Place sorting my poems
> in the rancid nourishment of this mountainous island
> they are coming and we holy ones must go
> is Tibet historically a part of China? as I historically
> belong to the enormous bliss of American death (325–26)

O'Hara confesses here that his chief desire is to be near death—not necessarily to die, but to achieve a state of transcendent knowledge and bliss. But the "holy" landscape in which he can experience such enlightenment is New York, not Tibet. O'Hara needs the "rancid nourishment" of Manhattan to feed his poetry, because in the city's continual process of creation and destruction "the enormous bliss of American death" finds its most dazzling expression. And just as Bud's joy is not caused by the patterns in the surf but in their passing, it is O'Hara's underlying awareness of death that illuminates and energizes his perception of his own life and his own desires.

Perhaps this is the kind of "deep gossip" that Allen Ginsberg is referring to in his elegy? But surely the phrase "curator of funny emotions to the mob" hardly does justice to the intensity and depth of a poem like "Rhapsody." One of the problems O'Hara's poetry has faced in gaining full recognition has been the common prejudice that a poet who likes bad Elizabeth Taylor movies, who inserts the names of his friends into poems, who quotes cab drivers, cannot possibly be as profound as the writing of great poetry demands.

Even now, O'Hara is still sometimes thought of as no more than a key figure in the "New York School" of poetry, a phrase facetiously adopted by the poets in O'Hara's circle to express their shared admiration for the New York painters. In the introduction to their *Anthology of New York Poets* (1970), poets David Shapiro and Ron Padgett remark that it would be "facile as well as misleading to see these poets as forming a 'School,'" but that, in fact, is how they are usually still categorized by people who cannot live without patterns.

Speaking of "schools" and "movements" never does justice to individual artists, especially of the caliber of Frank O'Hara, John Ashbery, Kenneth Koch, and James Schuyler. Yet, without suggesting that these poets ought to be considered as part of a group, it still might be worthwhile to list some of the qualities that have become associated with the "New York School," so that, as we proceed, we can see how O'Hara's poetry is related to it, but also transcends it. This will be illustrated with a few quotations from Padgett and Shapiro's anthology, which, despite the editors' disclaimer, does suggest a shared sensibility.[6]

As represented in the *Anthology of New York Poets*, these poets do not write for political, social or intellectual causes, nor do they write much about nature, except in an urban context:

> I wake
> and hear the steam pipe knock
> like a metal heart
> and find it has snowed.
>
> (James Schuyler, "A White City")

Or they see nature as an art work, created or improved by man:

> ... the land
> Was made of paper processed
> To look like ferns, or other
> Whose sea unrolled its magic
> Distances and then rolled them up
> Its secret was only a pocket.
>
> (John Ashbery, "Rivers and Mountains")

None of them is an especially "American" poet, although American culture, including kitsch and pop culture, finds its way into their poems.

> Father came in wearing his Dick Tracy necktie: "How about a
>   drink everyone?"
> I said, "Let's go outside a while." Then we went out onto the
>   porch and sat on the Abraham Lincoln swing.
> You sat on the eyes, mouth, and beard part, and I sat on the
>   knees.
>
> (Kenneth Koch, "You Were Wearing")

If love is a theme in the work of these poets, it is usually a love that has either mystified them or else mysteriously disappeared. None of them is much concerned with the family or marriage, except as bemused outsiders:

> They
> are a medium-sized couple who
> when they fold each other up
> well, thrill. That's their story.
>
> (James Schuyler, "Freely Espousing")

For these poets, the loss of youth and love does not constitute a tragic theme. The emotions of loneliness, fear, awe, jealousy, despair, guilt rarely enter their poems. They are not interested in the concept of the soul or the business of the soul. They are not interested in large-scale atrocities, nor have they any vision of an ideal society or a corrupted society. They are not concerned with death and violence except in its capacity for energizing language:

> a hunk of scrap iron
> just there on the turnpike
> for no reason
> flies up and
> whang
> it goes on your new underneath
> well, its like you were thrown
> grabbed by the scruff of the neck
>> (James Schuyler, "Stun")

Their personal histories, their origins or their parents, are not
recorded in their poetry. They are not concerned about the
"sterility" of America. Their poems never contain a message to
help us make some kind of moral order in our lives. They are
neither concerned with timeless values, nor with portraying
average, everyday reality. Instead, they are interested in the
colors and textures of life as momentary, isolated phenomena,
detached from intellectual, moral or religious pattern:

> ...A timeless value, has changed hands.
> And you could have a new automobile
> Ping pong set and garage, but the thief
> Stole everything like a miracle.
> In his book there was a picture of treason only
> And in the garden, cries and colors.
>> (John Ashbery, "Last Month")

What is left to them, then, is a poetry which creates a field of
play for language:

> One day the Nouns were clustered in the street.
> An Adjective walked by, with her dark beauty.
> The Nouns were struck, moved, changed.
> The next day a Verb drove up and created the Sentence.
>> (Kenneth Koch, "Permanently")

And the American language, especially the language of daily
usage and speech, is the hero—perhaps the comic hero—of their
poems:

> The sensuous beauty of words like allergy
> the tonic resonance of

pill when used as in
"she is a pill"

(James Schuyler, "Freely Espousing")

Such, at least, is what is often thought of as the general stance of the "New York School" poets. The problem for the critic in writing about O'Hara's work is to demonstrate its essential seriousness despite O'Hara's so-called "New York School" rejection of so many of the usually serious subjects and to convey an idea of this seriousness without being false to O'Hara's sense of playfulness, his spur-of-the-moment grace.

Unlike Ashbery, Koch, or Schuyler, O'Hara's primary achievement has been his use of himself in his own poems as something like the "visual-biographical emblem" that Pasternak speaks of. The central figure in O'Hara's poetry is himself; but unlike Montaigne, the man is not the book, and there are hints of depths that are never fully sounded. There are no extended childhood memories, no memories of past love affairs, in general, no history of the self at all. One gets to know O'Hara through a series of moments, and one of his constant themes is his perception of himself as an array of separate selves, multifarious and unpredictable, constantly creating himself anew as if he were himself a work of art. Yet the poet as he appears in his own poems does have a recognizable personality, and it might be helpful to try to form some sort of composite description of this figure.

The Frank O'Hara that O'Hara's own writings project has a strange double aspect. He is, as he said himself, both feminine and tough. His love-life is promiscuous, unpredictable, but he is rarely intentionally cruel, and never victimized. He is aware of a certain love of evil in himself which fascinates rather than disturbs him. His moods are often extreme. He hates most being inactive; always feels best when he is "in love" with someone. Love, as a permanent commitment to another male is not within his capability, but love, even seen as a temporary suspension of the usual law of human loss, means a great deal to him, as does friendship. He likes to pretend to be enthusiastic about marriage and terribly fond of happy couples, and forms deep and lasting friendships with women, sometimes of a flirty brother-and-sister kind. If he has ever physically loved a woman he never says so, and this and many other details of his past he does not discuss.

He has thought of himself as a homosexual ever since early adolescence, long enough not to be angry at himself for being different or ashamed of being unmanly, since he is not. "Better a faggot than a farthead" (441), as he once put it.

Even before he is a lover, the man O'Hara portrays for us as himself is a writer. Like most writers, he is much happier when he is writing. When he is not, he tends to drink and smoke more and becomes less affable and more critical. He gets his writing done on the spur of the moment usually, whenever there is time and inspiration, often during his two-hour lunch break from the Museum. He can sit down and write a poem with a party going on around him, with music blaring on the radio, and action and noise inspire him rather than disturb him. His attitude towards his poetry is one of extreme diffidence growing out of complete confidence in his own genius.

This is only a general sketch; much more can undoubtedly be learned about the man through a detailed study of his work. But, as he himself would have preferred, our inquiry will be concerned with the poems for their own sake, and only with his life as material he transformed into his poetry: "Do not watch over my life," O'Hara implores us, "but read and read through copper earth" (302).

CHAPTER 2

Language and Style

O'HARA'S poetry is innovative, but he disliked theorizing. His attitude toward the craft of poetry was that there ought not to be much. "You just go on your nerve," he explained. "I don't believe in god, so I don't have to make elaborately sounded structures. . . . I don't even like rhythm, assonance, all that stuff. . . . If someone's chasing you down the street with a knife you just run, you don't turn around and shout, 'Give it up! I was a track star for Mineola Prep.'" O'Hara goes on to say that as for "measure" and other technical matters in poetry "that's just common sense: if you're going to buy a pair of pants you want them to be tight enough so everyone will want to go to bed with you. There's nothing metaphysical about it" (498). Few poets, if any, have pretended to be so offhand about the technique of verse.

But even though such nonstatements tell us little about O'Hara's method as a poet, they do give us some account of the reasons O'Hara wrote the way he did. O'Hara rejected the possibility of metaphysical truth. Because he did not believe a poet should seek to impose order on experience, he did not want to impose the order of an elaborate, carefully wrought prosody on his own verse. But though O'Hara claims not to "like" poetic devices such as meter, rhyme, assonance and "all that stuff," he nevertheless does seek a kind of shapeliness, the verbal equivalent of "pants . . . tight enough so everyone will want to go to bed with you." He does not want to be correct, but he does want to be attractive. His humorous reference to the importance of running, rather than turning to face his pursuer and assert his credentials reflects his dislike for a language that asserts its own authority. Poetic language, he believed, ought to come spontaneously to mind under the stress of immediate experience.

45

The poet should not sound as though, through the authority of his carefully constructed verses, he has the power to escape the contingency of his life.

The truth that O'Hara is looking for in his poetry is an intimate truth. As O'Hara explains in his tongue-in-cheek manifesto, "Personism," the whole "movement" came into being "after lunch with LeRoi Jones on August 27, 1959, a day in which I was in love with someone. . . . I went back to work and wrote a poem for this person. While I was writing it I was realizing that if I wanted to I could use the telephone instead of writing the poem, and so Personism was born" (499). Though O'Hara is being facetious here—he never thought of "Personism" as a "movement," but only as an attitude that suited him in the writing of certain poems—what he is saying here has broad implications for his language. He wants the informal diction of the telephone rather than the verbal structure usually associated with the printed page. This desire reflects his interest in interpersonal truth and his rejection of the black and white truth of moral stricture. Yet O'Hara's poems do not merely reproduce talk; his innovations of language and style reflect a search for beauty and truth in everyday life.

Like Whitman, O'Hara makes use of as broad a poetic diction as possible, incorporating the details of his experience, no matter how homely or shocking. At times, O'Hara's poetic speech is the "queertalk" of homosexuals; when it is not, it is still, more generally, the language of a man who cares more about his feelings and his relationships than about moral or societal conventions. But while, for the most part, O'Hara's language is that of the everyday, of the interpersonal, it is also a poetic language seeking to confer heightened significance upon ordinary experience. Surreal, dreamlike images add a sense of aesthetic and psychological complexity; the poems are also infused with a sense of "design"—an attention to verbal surface that counteracts any tendency to fall into too-easy patterns of thought and feeling. O'Hara's poetic voice is not simply conversational, but extremely flexible. Through a subtle mixture of voices O'Hara is able to express the importance of the artist's calling without wrenching himself completely away from the language and facts of everyday life.

I *Wide-ranging Diction*

O'Hara's diction resembles an open-house party at which junkies and society matrons rub elbows. He welcomes all kinds of words into his poems—no matter how improper—and at the same time likes to include numerous references to low and high-brow culture and to friends and New York landmarks (both famous and obscure). Such diction has the effect of placing the poem within a personal domain. O'Hara can be shocking; he can also be obscurely private. But, in both cases, he is insisting that his poems will be like face-to-face communications—uninhibited, and grounded in his immediate milieu.

O'Hara seems to delight in including unusual, even improper items in his poems. "Ah! I know only too well how/ black my heart is," he writes, "how at home I am with snails/ and dingle-berries and // other dark things" ("A Proud Poem," 52). Like Whitman, O'Hara feels a compulsion to pay witness to the dark side of himself and, also like Whitman, tries to shock with his range. Sounding a bit like a learned street urchin, O'Hara begins a section in *Second Avenue*: "I come to you smelling of the shit of the Pyrrhian Maidens!" At times, though, his inclusiveness renders certain states of feeling and experiences with remarkable accuracy, and the shock is not so much one of impropriety but of recognition.

One such poem is "Blocks," which describes adolescence. Out of a melange of confusing verbal exuberance appear many details that readers are likely to remember from their own adolescence. For example, a reminder of what it feels like to be beaten up at school: "the cross-eyed tantrum-tousled ninth grader's/ splayed fist is freezing on the cement!" Or this reference to clandestine love and eating:

> Vivo! the dextrose
> those children consumed, lavished, smoked, in their knobby
> candy bars. Such pimples! such hardons! such moody loves.
> And thus they grew like giggling fir trees.   (108)

By including rarely-spoken-of details O'Hara has captured the sourness and awkwardness of adolescence and also the exhilaration of new-found desire and inexorable growth. As Helen

Vendler has pointed out in praising O'Hara's all-inclusive diction
in this poem: "Almost all other poems about adolescence have
concealed one or the other of these facets of the state, whether
out of shame or aesthetics one scarcely knows."[1] She goes on
to say that O'Hara's sometimes shocking, sometimes charming
devotion to details often neglected or thought unworthy to be
put into poems can serve as a "new source of truth." This was,
indeed, O'Hara's belief too. "Such things," he tells us in "Today,"
"are with us everyday/ . . . They/ do have meaning. They're as
strong as rocks" (15).

The problem with O'Hara's inclusiveness is that it can be
bewildering and trivial at times, especially with the proliferation
of names that comes in his later poetry. While Yeats, in one of
his greatest poems, could take a list of the names of Irish
revolutionary heroes and "write it out in verse" so that the men's
plain Irish names are the *source* of the high music of the poem,
illustrating their transformation from ordinary men into eternal
heroes in the history of the race—

> MacDonagh and MacBride
> And Connally and Pearse
> Now and in time to be,
> Wherever green is worn
>
> ("Easter, 1916")

—O'Hara, by comparison, seems to be making, not poems, but
pages in a scrapbook:

> Kupka buildings aren't being built, damn it
> and I'm locked up in this apartment outdoors for a good reason, Mario
> Mario? there are 20 of em in this neighborhood
>   in your blue sweater
>   excepting there's a staggering grid   of . . .
> air cooling, rushing along   out of the Astor
>   out of the Ritz, Godfrey
>   out of the Broadhurst-Plaza
>   I'll have an omelette aux fine herbes
>   like after *Dolce Vita*   (410)

Yet, at its best, O'Hara's inclusiveness creates a sense of a
crowded, busy, but familiar world. In "Adieu to Norman, Bon
Jour to Joan and Jean-Paul," for example, the poet tells us that

he is hurrying to write his poem in order to finish it for a specific luncheon party to celebrate one friend's departure, and two friends' arrival. His world is that of an urban coterie: he and the friends (for whom he is writing the poem) know hundreds of people in common. Their security in the midst of confusion and change resides in this shared world of names. Just as the streets of Paris that he has been looking up on his map have a kind of permanence (as much as anything in a city can have) so too he is reassured by the essential continuity of friendship. While it may be "Adieu" to Norman, it is at least "Bon Jour" to Joan and Jean-Paul.

Worried about whether his poems are "any good or not" and deciding that "the only decision you can make is that you did it" (that he and his work have to go on existing apart from questions of value) O'Hara is reassured by the collective testimony of Paris streets, museums, bars, parks, a host of friends and favorite writers, that "we shall continue to be ourselves." In "Adieu to Norman, Bon Jour to Joan and Jean-Paul" the abundance of names creates a crowded personal map that is, in itself, a representation of both the source of his anxiety and of his happiness. Though many of the people mentioned in O'Hara's poem happen to be well-known poets and artists, O'Hara is not saying as Yeats did that his friends will share a kind of glory and immortality. He implies, rather, that it is a fine thing simply to have as many friends as possible, so that within the confusion of their continual comings and goings there exists, however fragile, a world to inhabit.

II *"Queertalk"*

One of the many kinds of language O'Hara introduces into his poetry is "queertalk"—a pattern of speech characteristic of certain homosexuals. Such speech, in some ways, is related to the "feminine" speech patterns of women. It suggests that the poet and the reader are joined in a private understanding of the world that is set apart from the ordinary public rhetoric of "straight" society. The poet is placing his poem "between the two of us," between himself and the reader, creating a kind of gossipy intimacy, and a shared set of private values and truths that displace the false values of public speech.

Two critics who have focused on this element in O'Hara's work, Stuart Byron and Bruce Boone, each see the publication of the *Collected Poems* as a major step towards an openness of self-identification on the part of homosexuals. Byron claims that of fifty poets in a recent "authoritative anthology of postwar American poetry . . . 10 of them I knew from the grapevine to be gay, but only three have come out in print—Paul Goodman, Allen Ginsberg and . . . O'Hara, albeit speaking from the grave."[2]

More important than O'Hara's writing poems which make it possible to identify him as a homosexual is the frequently humorous and self-accepting way he manages to incorporate both homosexual lifestyle and language into his poems. As Stuart Byron explains, the difference between O'Hara and Allen Ginsberg on this point is that while Ginsberg acknowledges his homosexuality he speaks "hiptalk" rather than "queertalk"; "O'Hara (however) spoke and wrote 'queertalk.' His way of describing a beautiful spring evening is to say, 'it's the night like I love it all cruisy and nelly.' Fancying himself a god, he knows just what he wants a god to look like: 'I was made in the image of a sissy truck driver.'" Both Boone and Byron agree that compared to Allen Ginsberg's writings on homosexuality O'Hara's language is more typical of homosexual speech and practice. Boone feels that "O'Hara is a person who is part of what he describes" in homosexual life while "for Ginsberg it is linguistically obvious that he feels himself an outsider—outside, in every way, from the group of people he is describing."

Making an extremely suggestive observation about O'Hara's language in general, Boone goes on to say that "O'Hara's attitudes towards language . . . reveal themselves as gay especially in their basic unwillingness to take seriously the demands of official—bourgeois/straight—language." He concludes that for O'Hara, and for homosexuals in general, "it becomes satisfying to break the rules of language in the most frivolous ways: they are not our rules, but the rules of an oppressor."[3]

This is certainly an important point to bear in mind when considering O'Hara's many innovations and idiosyncracies of style. For now, though, it highlights at least one characteristic feature of O'Hara's poetic diction not previously mentioned, his tendency to consign certain expressions to quotation marks, as though to quote Boone, he is "borrowing" them temporarily from "official" language but wishes, essentially, to disassociate himself from them. Thus, in "Sudden Snow," for example, he puts part of the academic-sounding phrase "poetic style 'as we know it'" in quotation marks as though to suggest the impossibility of "knowing" such a complex thing collectively. O'Hara makes fun of (and reverses) the usual meaning of simplistic moral terms like "bad character":

> someone comes along with a very bad character
> he seems attractive. is he really. yes. very
> he's attractive as his character is bad. is it. yes . . .
>
> and you take a lot of dirt off someone
> is the character less bad. no. it improves constantly
> you don't refuse to breathe do you   (327)

The absence of a question mark makes the question about "bad character" flatly rhetorical; obviously, what is "bad" in the straight world is going to be "attractive" in the gay world. And the moral terminology of the establishment is reduced to so many labels.

Though it is tempting (and sometimes valid) to make connections between unconventional lifestyle and unconventional linguistic practices, we must do so cautiously. In "Essay on Style," for example, O'Hara is questioning the honesty of his mother's language:

> wouldn't you know my mother would call
> up
>   and complain?
>   my sister's pregnant and
> went to the country for the weekend without
> telling her
>   in point of fact why don't I
> go out to have dinner with her or "let her"
> come in?   (393)

The phrase "let her" implies that the son petulantly or even cruelly refuses the mother permission to come to see him. This places the blame on the son, rather than on the mother for trying to force an invitation, and as such O'Hara contemptuously holds

it up as an example of his mother's manipulative language. "No,"
O'Hara concludes, suddenly addressing his mother in the second
person, "I am not going/ to have you 'in' for dinner nor am I
going 'out'/ I am going to eat alone for the rest of my life"
(394). Here he seems to be undermining the validity of the
usual concepts of "in" and "out" as well as the practice of consistent pronoun reference. He feels close enough to his mother
to suddenly shift the poem into a message directed especially
to her—to "you"—yet he does not feel that such closeness comprises a true intimacy. Nothing feels intimate, not even his
own language. In this case, O'Hara is not so much a homosexual
at war with what Boone has called "the language of the oppressor," but a son at odds with his mother and his mother tongue.

At times, though, O'Hara does give his language feminine, if
not overtly homosexual overtones, and these can be important in
interpreting certain of his poems. In "Poem (Lana Turner has
collapsed)," for example, O'Hara's chattiness suggests the
associative language of women, or at least of stereotyped women
in movies:

> I was trotting along and suddenly
> it started raining and snowing
> and you said it was hailing
> but hailing hits you on the head
> hard so it was really snowing and
> raining and I was in such a hurry
> to meet you but the traffic
> was acting exactly like the sky
> and suddenly I see a headline
> LANA TURNER HAS COLLAPSED!   (449)

Perhaps we are to infer O'Hara's identification with Lana from
the breathless, scatterbrained, feminine voice of the poem. At
any rate, Lana's collapse is an evil omen to O'Hara—as is the
bad weather and the confused traffic—and prefigures the possibility of some personal disaster. "I have been to lots of parties,"
O'Hara concludes, "and acted perfectly disgraceful/ but I never
actually collapsed." But if Lana Turner can collapse, so might he:
"oh Lana Turner we love you get up." With his all-in-one-breath
syntax, and the shifting pronouns (from "I" to "you" to "we")

O'Hara pulls the reader into his comical, panicky anecdote, and suggests a certain hyperemotional vulnerability. Since he does not understand the causes of events, he must rely on intimacy, wishfulness, and love.

III *Surreal Imagery*

Though "Poem (Lana Turner has collapsed)" is chatty, it is important to note that because of its seemingly haphazard conversational language a strange shift of time and place occurs. Is O'Hara with his friend, or rushing to meet him? "You said it was hailing," O'Hara recalls, but then says "I was in such a hurry to meet you." Probably he means that later, when the two of them were together, they discussed the weather. But, for the moment, the time order of the narrative has been strangely warped. This adds to the over-all sense of humorous but threatening confusion: O'Hara is seen as a man adrift in the flow of things.

Often O'Hara makes use of the disorderliness of conversational speech to create a feeling of dreamlike displacement. He also uses surreal, fantasy images. At best, such techniques give everyday events and scenes a strangeness that increases their suggestiveness. Yet at other times, especially in his earlier poetry, what John Ashbery called O'Hara's "home-grown Surrealism" (x) can make his poems practically incoherent. In "Original Sin," for example, we encounter:

> Dense black trees trapped and bound! the hairy skull
> and pushed wildly against the door of sky!
> the paralyzed flowers, ah! with each eye
> shrieking, caught in the web of stars, skillful
>
> seiners! in the pitiless sea of will.
> Hysterical telegraph vines cry to
> the vacationing sky, monstrous! the blue
> mother with her breasts to the wall. . . .   (48)

Without the title to suggest the stricken landscape of Eden, and Eve "the blue mother," these images would whirl by without any apparent connection. Even so, the imagery is overly abstract and phantasmagoric. If the poem had another title—say, "Florida"

—it would have another meaning. One might think of an old
vacationer dying, the hysterical telegrams to the children. . . .

But when O'Hara uses this technique to add richness of texture
and dream overtones to his descriptions of all-too-familiar situations, he is able to make strong poems out of subjects that are
ordinarily thought unworthy of being rendered in verse. For
example, in "An Abortion," O'Hara's rapid shifts from fact
to metaphor, from narrative to surreal dream image adds emotional complexity to what would otherwise be a poignant
but banal topic. Compassion for the unborn fetus may well turn
into sentimentality since the fetus, though potentially human,
is also prehuman and unknowable. O'Hara, however, avoids
slipping too patently into easy sympathy by splicing together
a complex montage of images, some of which seem drawn from
actual events, others from fantasy:

> Do not bathe her in blood,
> the little one whose sex is
> undetermined, she drops leafy
> across the belly of black
> sky and her abyss has not
> that sweetness of the March
> wind. Her conception ached
> with the perversity of nursery
> rhymes, she was a shad a
> snake a sparrow and a girl's
> closed eye. At the supper, weeping,
> they said let's have her and
> at breakfast: no.   (80–81)

O'Hara's imagery puts us sympathetically inside the womb with
the fetus, but only gradually allows us to see her as human.
She evolves, first, from leaf, to shad, to snake, to sparrow, and
then—the final image in the list—to a "girl's closed eye," but
never to a baby. She is not a sweet little thing, but a creature
headed for death, conceived originally out of some perverse
sentimentality about children and childish things. The emotional
suspension created by these images enables O'Hara to shift suddenly but logically to a fragment of narrative where the parents
are deciding the baby's fate—first with sentimental weeping,
and then with cold decisiveness. It is not right to bathe the baby

in blood, nor in tears—neither to kill her, nor to pity her. This leads to the poem's final paradoxical ambivalence: "From our tree/ dropped, that she not wither,/ autumn in our terrible breath." The act of abortion may save the fetus from later "withering" at the hands of unloving parents, but it is also an act of terrifying destruction. These two opposed feelings are linked together syntactically, just as they are emotionally inseparable.

IV *Verse Design*

Whether O'Hara is writing experimental verse or conventionally (along the left margin), or with "open" typography (arranging his lines over the page), his best poems have an overall sense of poetic "design."

For O'Hara, "form" refers to the shape of thought within the poem, while "design" refers to the shape and sound of the words. Just as a poem can be formless, mere emotional ranting, so too it can be "smothered " in form when it follows a conventional pattern of thought. "Design," O'Hara declared, "is the point where the poet can hold his ground in the impasse between formal smothering and emotional spilling over" (SS, 35).

Though design often undercuts excessive emotion, as O'Hara suggests, it also replenishes emotion by preventing the poem from drowning in artless sentimentality. At its best, O'Hara's verse design intensifies and complicates thought and feeling in his poems, and this complexity enables him to transcend his often quite unpretentious materials. The design of his verses may also aid him in achieving a higher tone when his subject demands it.

O'Hara searched for unusual methods of introducing a sense of design into his poetry, but some of his playful experiments are more odd than they are successful. Surveying the *Collected Poems* one encounters prose poems, sonnets, acrostics, a poem whose last thirty-three lines all end with the word "of" ("Night and Day in 1952"), a poem in the shape of a face, another in the form of a saw, and a poem where the rhymes fall at the beginning of the line ("Goodbye to Great Spruce Head Island"). At times we can only wonder at the intrepidity with which O'Hara pursues his experiments, as in "Dream of Berlin" where he ends each line with a word in parentheses and the (disconcerting)

effect is something like that of two unrelated blurps of electronic
music coming from speakers in different places:

> these (hairs)
> are the soldiers (armor)
> of Fidelio (dark)
> Yoicks! (feet)
> hunting in the abyss (parade)   (320)

At other times, however, O'Hara's experiments can be interesting and well-executed, and display impressive resourcefulness.
In the early typographical experiment "Poem (WHE EWHEE)"
he follows the outline of his friend Jane Freilicher's face. The
resulting picture poem is much more intricate than any of
Apollinaire's in *Calligrams*, and the zaniness of the design seems
well-suited to O'Hara's playful taunting praise for Jane's talent
and beauty.

Design can be aural too, and in one of O'Hara's best experimental poems a playful use of rhyme enables him to move im-
perceptibly from silliness to bliss. As John Ashbery has said, any
poet who could write "At night Chinamen jump/ on Asia with
a thump" in the academic atmosphere of the 1940's was "amusing himself" and engaged in a "highly suspect activity" (viii).
Chinamen here are, of course, not Chinese but something like
fantasy figures on bedroom wallpaper or illustrations from old
social studies textbooks. At first in "Poem (At night Chinamen
jump)" sex is seen as a form of play ("affectionate games") and
the rhymes give the impression that the poet is carried away by
his delightful song and could not care less about Asia or sex. But
this playful design produces a delicate surprise at the end of the
poem. O'Hara begins by linking together through rhyme two
subjects that seem remote from one another—

> At night Chinamen jump
> on Asia with a thump
>
> while in our willful way
> we, in secret, play   (13)

—as though suggesting that the erotic connection between people
most often begins in play, not in seriousness. But by the end

of the poem the "willful" children seem to have discovered sex in earnest, and the subjects which seemed unlinkable have become truly joined: "Chinese rhythms beat/ through us in our heat." O'Hara's rich use of sound—as in "a heath// full of Chinese thrushes/ flushed from China's bushes" (14)—intensifies the poem as it blossoms from a mere nursery rhyme into a beguiling love lyric.

Until about 1957 O'Hara's usual practice in verse design was to line up his poems along the left margin and to use what seem to be arbitrary enjambments. Sometimes, as in "How Roses Get Black," the line breaks imply a typographical irony and act as an emotional damper. It is as though the poet is reminding us that he is, just as he claims to be, amused, aloof, and in control—"I,// who can cut with a word."

At other times, even in a very good poem like "A True Account of Talking to the Sun at Fire Island," the line breaks seem simply careless, as though the poet is seeking an unpretentious, offhand, unskilled look to match the informality of the diction:

> "Frankly I wanted to tell you
> I like your poetry. I see a lot
> on my rounds and you're okay. You may
> not be the greatest thing on earth, but
> you're different. . . ."   (306)

Yet at other times the line breaks can help emphasize both sound and sense. This is particularly likely to happen at the end of a poem where O'Hara wants to modulate from conversational diction and seemingly arbitrary line breaks to verse that is slightly heightened in tone and more sound-rich. In "My Heart," O'Hara concludes:

> . . . I wear workshirts to the opera,
> often. I want my feet to be bare,
> I want my face to be shaven, and my heart—
> you can't plan on the heart, but
> the better part of it, my poetry, is open.   (231)

The word "often" is echoed by the strange word "shaven" and

by "open"; "heart" rhymes with "part"; after the little run of *p*
sounds "open" seems to turn "poetry" inside out, aurally emphasizing O'Hara's message: the poem must be both open and poetic,
free of the wrought quality that verse often has, but at the
same time elevated, when appropriate, above the merely random
sounds of prose.

In one of the best poems from O'Hara's early career, "The
Hunter," O'Hara uses enjambments to establish a rhythm of
ironic disappointment. The hunter (perhaps the humble chamois
hunter of Byron's *Manfred*) seems to be hunting for the very
thing he ought not to want to find. O'Hara, using enjambments,
creates the mocking effect of tedious and futile effort: "he set out
and kept hunting/ and hunting. Where, he thought/ and
thought, is the real chamois?" Each new line here begins with
an old phrase, suggesting a journey that gets the hunter nowhere.
Falling leaves seem "like pie plates," manna falls from the
sky, a woman's face appears momentarily in the clouds, but
nature does not after all mean to be a kind, nurturing mother to
him. The poem ends with the same pattern of repetition with
which it began, as though the hunter's end could have been
foreseen at the beginning of his futile quest:

> He thought, why did I come? and then,
> I have come to rule! The chamois came.
>
> The chamois found him and they came
> in droves to humiliate him. Alone,
> in the clouds, he was humiliated.   (167)

By placing the quiet but ominous announcement "The chamois
came" in the same line with the hunter's brief moment of kingly
pride, O'Hara speeds up the hunter's tragedy and creates an
effect of droll pathos. The penultimate line nicely balances the
"droves" of chamois against the poor hunter who is "Alone."
The final line, "in the clouds, he was humiliated," emphasizes
both the hunter's height and the extent of his delusion, and by
repeating "humiliated" O'Hara introduces a sense of almost
biblical inevitability and finality. The chamois "came . . . to
humiliate him," and "he was humiliated" indeed. The greatest

humiliation, the poem tells us, is having the truth in front of us from the very beginning and not seeing it.

In his early poetry, O'Hara often uses abundant exclamation points in order to incorporate contradictory moods into a single stanza:

> . . . I raced to the door.

> "Come back" I cried "for a minute!
> You left your new shoes. And the
> coffee pot's yours!" There were no
> footsteps. Wow! what a relief!   ("A Rant," 54)

In the poems from 1957 on, many of which have an "open" typographical manner, O'Hara has a way of visually separating statements in the poem which have to carry separate emotional charges:

> YIPPEE! I'm glad I'm alive
>   "I'm glad you're alive
> too, baby, because I want to fuck you"
>   ("Ode to Michael Goldberg," 294)

O'Hara's later manner projects conflicts of voice and tone visually, without depending as much on punctuation. He seems to want us to be aware of that "YIPPEE!" suspended on the page as if jumping for joy, above that very down-to-earth reply.

On the other hand, the shape of the poem can often be dictated by visual aesthetic demands. The poem with "open" design is not just written, it is sculpted. In "Ode to Michael Goldberg," for example, the passage beginning "So I left, the stars were shining" makes a pleasingly tranquil column of type to contrast visually with the agitated, scattered verses that precede it. The "shape" or design of the passage can in turn influence tone.

One of the attractive features of O'Hara's *Odes,* published in an extremely large format interspersed with colorful, spattery serigraphs by Mike Goldberg, is the interesting and varied patterns of type on the page. In "Ode: Salute to the French Negro Poets," in long lines reminiscent of Whitman's self-published first edition of *Leaves of Grass* (O'Hara calls Whitman his

"great predecessor" at the beginning of the ode) O'Hara writes
one of his most sombre and public poems. In a voice that is rare
for him he speaks for America:

the beauty of America, neither cool jazz nor devoured Egyptian
                            heroes, lies in
lives in the darkness I inhabit in the midst of sterile millions

the only truth is face to face, the poem whose words become
                            your mouth
and dying in black and white we fight for what we love, not are
                                                              (305)

The characteristics of O'Hara's usual voice are still very much
in evidence here (the wonderful revision in midthought "lies in/
lives in" and the witty reference to biracial struggle as "dying in
black and white") but the voice is more elevated and noble than
usual. The long lines, which give the poem the look of a
monument inscription, emphasize this and, indeed, may have
helped to bring it about.

V   Mixed Voices

Though O'Hara usually writes with informal diction about his
immediate, everyday world, his language rises at times to a more
heightened tone, particularly when his theme is the role of art
and the artist. Yet he is able to control his poetic voice so that,
while it may modulate to a more elevated language, it never
separates itself completely from his usual more modest and conversational manner of speech.

In "Poem (There I could never be a boy)," an account of a
poet's psychological initiation and coming of age, O'Hara com-
bines the simple, concrete language of the boy with the more
elevated and spiritual language of the mature poet. "At a cry
from mother," he tells us, "I fell to my knees!/ there I fell,
clumsy and sick and good." Only a boy would use "good" as it is
used here, as something worse than either "clumsy" or "sick."
And in the midst of this intense account of the boy-poet's self-
emancipation O'Hara breaks the heightened lyrical diction and
the galloping momentum of the poem with a little joke about the

mother's overprotectiveness: "All things are tragic/ when a mother watches!"

The poet achieves a mastery of life despite his mother's wish to be all things to him—to humiliate and to inspire him. The mare the boy rides is spurred upward by fright and pain, and the mother wishes that she could replace the mare in her son's terrifying adventure and feel "the random fears of a scarlet soul, as it breathes in and out/ and nothing chokes or breaks from triumph to triumph." The language here blends the spiritual and the physical as if while the mature poet is describing the sexual exaltation and terror of the journey, the boy notes that, despite his mother's overanxiety, "nothing chokes or breaks."

The use of "green" to describe the boy-poet, and the image of his riding to maturity will remind many readers of Dylan Thomas's beautiful "Fern Hill." O'Hara's diction is neither as sound-rich nor as striking as Thomas's but is more appropriate to a child's growing consciousness. In Thomas's poem, the sensibility may be that of a child, but the diction is that of a mature poet seeking to incorporate a child's imaginativeness into his verse. In O'Hara's poem, a true poem of adolescence, the child's diction coexists with that of the adult:

> I knew her but I could not be a boy,
> for in the billowing air I was fleet and green
> riding blackly through the ethereal night
> towards men's words which I gracefully understood,
>
> and it was given to me
> as the soul is given the hands
> to hold the ribbons of life!
> as miles streak by beneath the moon's sharp hooves
> and I have mastered the speed and strength which is the
> armor of the world.   (217)

Beginning with a line of monosyllabic words, the first stanza here modulates into "adult" diction (with adjectives like "billowing" and "ethereal") and then subsides back into the child's voice almost completely, except for the adverb "gracefully." This modulation of voice from that of the child to that of the adult and then into a unique combination of the two, mimics the leap into adulthood taken by an adolescent who nevertheless still

retains some of the consciousness of a child. The reins of the
chariot are seen by him as "ribbons," and he expresses himself
in the concrete, plain analogies of a child's mind: "and it was
given to me/ as the soul is given the hands." At the end of the
poem the poet has become both the mare ("*I* was fleet and
green") and the rider, embodying within himself both male and
female sources of inspiration, while the diction reminds us continually that he has the characteristics of both the child and
the adult.

O'Hara's best poem on a public political issue, "Answer to
Voznesensky and Evtushenko," provides us with a final example
of the upper range of O'Hara's voice. In his reply to the Russian
poets, O'Hara demonstrates visually the kind of flexibility that
he is accusing the Russians of not having:

> where you see death
>   you see a dance of death
>   which is
> imperialist, implies training, requires techniques
> our ballet does not employ

The wit here is that of a cultivated man who can savor the irony
of a "revolutionary" society which fosters only the traditional
ballet of the Imperial Court. But while upholding the greater
flexibility and freedom of American dance and art, O'Hara is
not an apologist for American society. He is merely arguing that
presuming to see a foreign country better than its own people
makes for clumsy thinking and clumsy poetry. He tells the
Russians:

> our selves are in far worse condition than the obviousness
> of your color sense
>   your general sense of Poughkeepsie is
> a gaucherie no American poet would be guilty of in Tiflis
> thanks to French Impressionism
>   we do not pretend to know more
> than can be known   (468)

Wittily rhyming "gaucherie" with "Poughkeepsie," and contrasting racist separatism with Impressionism's "color sense" (no pure
black and white, only blends of colors), the voice of the poem

asserts that refinement of feeling is not solely a European trait. It mixes hometown informality and pride with a sophisticated respect for European culture. O'Hara is asking for refinement of vision and, above all, a tolerance that hesitates to interfere in other's lives. To interfere, especially to do so crudely, denies the full humanity of those we criticize, and possibly sacrifices our own humanity as well. In the Russian poets' bungling attempt to use political influence, O'Hara concludes, we can see nothing better or more dignified than "Mayakovsky's hat worn by a horse."

O'Hara's language, with its "democratic diction," abundance of proper names, "queertalk" and feminine chattiness, is primarily the language of a poet who wishes to restrict his focus to his own milieu and to personal relationships. But he is capable of considerable resourcefulness in imagery, design, and tone. Unlike the Russians, he himself does not "pretend to know more/ than can be known," but writes about what can be known and what can be felt with subtlety and authority.

CHAPTER 3

Coherence

IN "Why I Am Not A Painter," O'Hara supplies us with an amusing but important anecdote about the unpredictability of the creative act. The question raised in the title is quickly abandoned; O'Hara says he would rather be a painter, but he is not. Yet the rest of the poem illustrates the similarity of his own method of composition with that of an Abstract Expressionist painter. He drops by Mike Goldberg's studio one day when Mike is starting a painting:

> "Sit down and have a drink" he
> says. I drink; we drink. I look
> up. "You have SARDINES in it."
> "Yes, it needed something there."
> "Oh." I go and the days go by
> and I drop in again. The painting
> is going on, and I go, and the days
> go by. I drop in. The painting is
> finished. "Where's SARDINES?"
> All that's left is just
> letters, "It was too much," Mike says.
>
> But me? One day I am thinking of
> a color: orange. I write a line
> about orange. Pretty soon it is a
> whole page of words, not lines.
> Then another page. There should be
> so much more, not of orange, of
> words, of how terrible orange is
> and life. Days go by. It is even in
> prose, I am a real poet. My poem
> is finished and I haven't mentioned
> orange yet. It's twelve poems, I call

it ORANGES. And one day in a gallery
I see Mike's painting, called SARDINES.   (261–62)

The tone of "Why I Am Not A Painter" indicates a humorous acceptance of the demands of creative work. Mike begins with a word and ends up with a design; O'Hara begins with a color and ends up with a poem. The work creates itself according to its own serendipitous will. (The poem seems to "drop in" on O'Hara in the same casual way that O'Hara drops in on Mike Goldberg.) But in allowing his poem to follow its own course, O'Hara discovers with feigned naiveté that he is a "real poet" after all. Art follows a higher sense of order and form than the artist could ever consciously impose upon it. "It was too much," says Mike, unable or unwilling to explain more precisely why he took out "SAR-DINES." "My poem/ is finished," says O'Hara even though he has not yet mentioned orange. The work seems to complete itself, and all the artist can or wants to explain about it is when and how it got done, but not its logic or formal structure.

In this chapter I want to explore the various degrees of coherence that can be found in O'Hara's poetry, especially in his longer poems. O'Hara's method for the longer poems is to keep the poem "open" so that, as with "Oranges," the subject of the poem is never quite circumscribed and the poem never quite arrives at any formal completion or thematic statement. (The implication is that the theme would be banal anyway, something like "how terrible orange is/ and life.") O'Hara wishes to find methods of composition that imitate the accidental nature of experience. But he also hopes to achieve a sense of aesthetic wholeness. In order to keep the poem "open" but at the same time give it some degree of coherence, O'Hara makes use of interwoven images and motifs. ("Oranges," for example, is linked together by a background color.)

In O'Hara's earliest long poem, "Second Avenue," it is the high-speed change of city life that seems to generate the poem. While "Second Avenue" consciously avoids recurrence, O'Hara's long poems of the late 1950's—"In Memory of My Feelings," "Ode to Michael Goldberg ('s Birth and Other Births)," "Ode on Causality," and others—are given internal coherence through recurring images.

In the short, first person narrative poems O'Hara referred to

as his " 'I do this I do that'/ poems" (341) O'Hara recounts
a series of events which leads to a crystalization of insight and
feeling. Even if only loosely and provisionally, such a crystalization seems to form the preceding details into a coherent
narrative.

The poems written in the 1960's generally follow either of two
patterns. In the love poems O'Hara's feelings confer a simple
unity of statement. As if aware that this coherence is caused by
a happy illusion, O'Hara comments: "everything is too comprehensible" (356). Though it is a source of temporary happiness
and security, love oversimplifies. After the love poems, O'Hara
seems to return to the technique of rapid transitions that he
employs in "Second Avenue," writing poems made up of
unrelated and often incomplete thoughts and events—often fragmented and trivial—as if his desire to organize experience disappears when love is no longer the theme. But even here, as the
doctrine of Abstract Expressionism maintains, the artist's unpre-
meditated gestures may often be right. O'Hara's final long poem,
"Biotherm," presents a restless, seemingly chaotic surface, but
one that is unified by motifs and a characteristic tone.

Let us examine several of the longer poems and some typical
shorter poems to illustrate the varying degrees of coherence
that can be found in O'Hara's work and to arrive at detailed
readings.

I "Second Avenue"

O'Hara makes his most ambitious exploration of the principle
of discontinuity in his long poem, "Second Avenue." This poem
which marks an extreme that he never again resorts to serves as
the purest example of the kind of rapid motion and surprising
transitions that characterize his poetry.

In commenting on "Second Avenue" O'Hara wrote: ". . . I
don't think [its meaning] can be paraphrased (or at least I hope
it can't)." The only organizing principle that O'Hara suggests is
that "everything . . . either happened to me or I felt happening
(saw, imagined) on Second Avenue" (495). But this provides
very broad boundaries for the poem indeed, since nearly anything can be "imagined" on Second Avenue. As for what is

"seen," the transitions are so sudden that most images are lifted out of context and their sources remain unclear.

For an analogy to this method we might consider Larry Rivers's explanation of the origins of the shapes in his painting *Second Avenue with THE* in the interview that he gave O'Hara for *Horizon* magazine.[1] The painting, to most viewers, would appear to be an urban abstraction, but for Rivers each line and splash of color had its origin in something that was in his field of vision at the time he was painting. Rivers's term for this kind of displacement of images is "smorgasbord of the recognizable" (*AC*, 118). On his canvas, the dark vertical lines painted across what seems to be the blue facade of a building are, in reality, the floorboards of the studio, and the lines of white squares in the upper right (where the fourth floor of the building seems to be shaping itself) are, as Rivers explains it, the keys of a piano he happened to have in the studio at the time. In O'Hara's "Second Avenue," too, what is "seen" may be the origin of the image, but the poem is highly abstracted, so that its source is usually concealed through strange juxtapositions and displacements.

O'Hara's most helpful remark about the structure of "Second Avenue" is his explanation of why the poem is dedicated to the poet Vladimir Mayakovsky and was influenced by the painter Willem de Kooning: "Mayakovsky and de Kooning ... both have done works as big as cities where the life in the work is autonomous (not about actual city life) and yet similar." "Second Avenue," then, is a work designed to have an autonomous life. It is not about the city, but it is *like* a city. Ultimately, the poem's true subject is its own surface, "high and dry, not wet, reflective and self-conscious." It was O'Hara's hope that the poem would "*be* the subject, not just about it" (497).

If there is a central statement in this poem for which all the rest provides a context, it occurs in the last section where O'Hara calls the city "the most substantial art product of our times." The city is a man-made world, artificial, and hence an "art product." A hyacinth, in this poem, is not a flower, or even a symbol of innocence as in T. S. Eliot's "Waste Land," but a telephone exchange: "HYacinth 9-9945." A season, in the world of "Second Avenue," is more likely to be "the season of the New York Ballet company" than any of the natural seasons.

Anticipating paintings by Rivers and by Robert Rauschenberg
that incorporate signs and pieces of newspaper, "Second Avenue"
records advertisements like "Same Day Cleaning" and headlines
like "WITHER ACCEPTED AS SELLING," and the names of
ordinary shops like "Dairy B&H Lunch" and "Majestic Camera
Store." But more important than the mere inclusion of such
fragments of the city's linguistic surface is O'Hara's application
of the principle of confusion and surprise. A poem that is
meant to resemble a city should, rightly, be unpredictable and
startling. We should not know, and we do not know, what is
coming up next in "Second Avenue." The language is full of
sudden changes of tone, and it shifts into other languages: a
passage from a French newspaper, phrases of Spanish, and even
Latin. But the clashing of these elements should not be made
too obvious either, lest the city be reduced to the travelogue
formula: Land of Contrasts. Instead, what has to exist in a poem
that resembles a city is some sense of the endless variety of
its elements and the way in which they refuse to be forced into
a pattern.

At one point O'Hara begins numbering his images, a technique which seems appropriate in this copious poem where
images rapidly follow one another without leading into one
another:

You are too young to remember the lack of snow in 1953 showing:
"1 Except that you react like electricity to a chunk of cloth,
it will disappear like an ape at night. 2 Before eating
there was a closing of retina against retina, and ice,
telephone wires! was knotted, spelling out farce
which is germane to lust. 3 Then the historic duel in the surf
when black garments were wasted and swept over battlements
into the moat. 4 The book contained a rosary pressed
in the shape of a tongue. 5 The hill had begun to roll
luminously. A deck appeared among the fir trees. Larry's
uncle sent a missionary to India when he was in grade school
who cried 'Go straight' to the white men there. Forgiveness
of heat. 6 Green lips pressed his body like a pearl shell.
7 It all took place in darkness, and meant more earlier
when they were in different places and didn't know each other.
As is often misprinted." And such whiteness not there!
All right, all right, all right, you glass of coke, empty

your exceptionally neonish newspaper from such left hands
with headlines to be grey as cut WITHER ACCEPTED AS SELLING.
(144)

The achievement here is very nearly the reverse of what we
usually look for in a poem; it lies in the degree of incoherence
that the poet is able to maintain. The poem comments on its own
disjointed surface, not only by listing and numbering its
images, but with references throughout to confusion and dis-
connection, as in: ". . . they were in different places and didn't
know each other." Consciousness in this poem does not flow or
stream but is constantly reacting to new shocks. Exclamations
break into the syntax—"Before eating/ there was a closing of
retina against retina, and ice,/ telephone wires! was knotted.
. . ." The exclamation "telephone wires!" intrudes into the
sentence, which then turns out to have crumbled apart anyway.
The consciousness here is a newborn consciousness—"You are
too young to remember the lack of snow in 1953" (the poem was
being written in 1953)—and is utterly distractible, so that even
the sentence is at times too long a span during which to maintain
continuity. This passage, like the rest of the poem, is saturated
with disappearance, transformation and flux. It is the "lack of
snow" that cannot be remembered; "it will disappear like an ape
in the night"; black garments are "wasted" and swept away; the
rosary becomes a tongue; hills roll; "it meant more earlier";
things are "often misprinted"; ". . . such whiteness *not there!*";
even "WITHER," whoever or whatever that is, is "SELLING."
Everything will disappear or change unless the poet can "react
like electricity," with lightning speed.

Reading "Second Avenue" is an unusual and bewildering experience, a "difficult pleasure" as John Ashbery puts it (ix).
Its most powerful and satisfying effect is its speed and energy.
Not only is the poem charged with verbs, but its unpredictable
transitions give it the fascination of dazzling movement. For
example, this vertiginous "run-on" question:

is it not the deepest glitterings of love when the head
is turned off, glancing over a stranger's moonlike hatred
and finding an animal kingdom of jealousy in parachutes
descending upon the highway which you are not speeding down?
(141)

The sensation of speed is increased by the many references to travel and flying, such as: " ... I'm blazoned and scorched like a fleet of windbells down the Pulaski Skyway" (150).

"Second Avenue" is ultimately an impressive testament to the endurance of O'Hara's imagination, and his ability to generate a kind of poetic perpetual motion. Like the flier he mentions at one point, the poet plays "on and on and on" and can "never go back" (143). We feel (and fear) that he could probably go on forever, but with the phrase "immobility forging an entrail from the pure obstruction of the air" O'Hara concludes the poem by simply stopping its motion.

All this motion—and the resulting lack of clear situations and scenes—is also responsible for the poem's wearisome impenetrability. In general, the long poems that he wrote after "Second Avenue" have more defined subjects, and communicate in a more distinctive and personal voice. "Second Avenue" is a one-of-a-kind creation which not only establishes a new concept of poetry but also finishes it off by exhausting its energy.

II *"Ode to Michael Goldberg"*

The difference between "Second Avenue" and "Ode to Michael Goldberg ('s Birth and Other Births)" can be seen most quickly by looking for a moment at the language of each before examining the different organizational principles they employ. The tough, resistant surface of "Second Avenue" gives way to a more intimate, more accessible language of the later poem. In "Second Avenue" the diction is often Latinate; it is often almost impossible to guess the tone of voice in which the poem should be read. We are often likely to feel subjected to a barrage of words. In the later poem, an "I" begins to address us in the opening lines. Unlike the supernatural "I" of "Second Avenue" who is the perceiving consciousness of the poem but not its subject, the "I" now becomes the subject, acquires a personality and speaks to us in the distinctive vernacular that we recognize as O'Hara's characteristic voice.

John Ashbery, in his introduction to the *Collected Poems*, identifies a new style emerging in O'Hara's poetry in the late 1950's, a style which is capable of changing the methods of organization and construction of the longer poems: "Though a conversational tone had existed in his poetry from the beginning, it had often seemed a borrowed one.... It was not yet a force that could penetrate the monolithic slipperiness of the long poems, breaking up their Surreal imagery and partially plowing it under to form in the process a new style incorporating the suggestions and temptations of every day as well as the dreams of the Surrealists" (x). The relaxed, conversational tone of certain passages in "Ode to Michael Goldberg" would not have been suitable for the incessant, lightning transitions—the "high and dry" surface—of "Second Avenue." On the other hand, a long poem written entirely in a relaxed tone would not be capable of building towards an eloquent climax. For this reason, poems like "In Memory of My Feelings" and "Ode to Michael Goldberg" have a kind of variable density; they are sometimes chatty, sometimes spare, at other times epigrammatic, or even expansively eloquent. In addition to a greater variation of tone, there are also a considerable variety of line arrangements and a lighter more penetrable surface, unlike the monolith of "Second Avenue," with its uniformly long lines.

The language becomes more explicit with more exposition and narrative; the poem begins to acquire a central theme, and often a continuing motif or series of motifs which can be associated with this theme. The way both "In Memory of My Feelings" and "Ode to Michael Goldberg" use chains of images is strongly reminiscent of musical composition. What seems like a passing and casual image, "warm as roses in the desert," from "In Memory of My Feelings," may turn out to be a motif linking up with Arabs, camels, sand, "the burnoose of memories," and so on. References to Stravinsky in both poems put one in mind of that composer's belief that almost any musical phrase, no matter how unlikely or startling, can serve as a theme or motif if it is repeated enough. That surely is O'Hara's belief as well, as he converts what often seem to be merely casual images into motifs by recollecting or echoing them. Working against the Surrealist principle of startling, arbitrary images is the principle of recurring motifs, and the reader's imagination is at once both taken by surprise and reassuringly controlled. "Warm as roses in the desert" may surprise him, popping up as it does without previous mention of the desert or explanation of why roses

are growing there, but by the time the other Arabian material
has been introduced the reader will begin to feel oriented.

These motifs are not necessarily symbols. We can guess, for
example, that (Arabic) numerals are important in a poem like
"In Memory of My Feelings" because we often retain certain
numbers and dates in order to recall and arrange memories:
"My 10 my 19/ my 9, and the several years. My/ 12 years since
they all died" (254). But far from being defined for us by the
poem, the meanings of these motifs are only suggested and
remain indefinite. So too, in "Ode to Michael Goldberg," horses
form a motif although not always suggesting the same idea, as
many of the references to horses are incidental or oblique. For
example: "a fleece of pure intention sailing like/ a pinto in a
barque of slaves." Or even more indirect: "cayuse meannesses."
It is as if O'Hara sank a shaft into his memories and kept coming up with horses, but did not want to define his associations
so strictly as to make horses a symbol. It is O'Hara's mastery of
precisely this technique, his ability to bring back an image or to
make his images resonate with each other, to connect them as
motifs rather than define them as symbols, that enables his
poetry to be both satisfyingly unified and ultimately indefinable
and abstract.

"Ode to Michael Goldberg" conveys a strong sense of thematic
unity despite its episodic array of scenes and images. Just as
"In Memory of My Feelings" is saturated with images of multiple
identity, the "Ode" is dominated by references to methods of
transportation—trails, highways, railroads, ships, automobiles,
bicycles, trucks, and horses—which point toward the central
theme of the poem: the motion of life itself. Birth is not a once-
in-a-lifetime experience but a continual process of departure. The
transportation images and references suggest the metaphor of
the life-journey, and the poem is unified by its continual emphasis
on movement.

Of the various movements in life, the poem includes: movement from place to place (as in the train trip that O'Hara took
from coast to coast during W.W. II, or the ship voyage in the
Pacific); being "moved" by love ("I'd sail with you anywhere");
the movement of the wind which sounds like Stravinsky and
which teaches O'Hara to recognize "art/ as wildness"; the movement toward death ("death belonging to another/ and suddenly

inhabited by you without permission/ you moved compulsively
and took it up"); the movement of growth which reminds him
of a political movement ("to be young and to grow bigger/ more
and more cells like germs/ or a political conspiracy"); and the
movement of flying, which seems to represent the act of writing
poetry. In addition, the poem is charged with activity. From the
very beginning, life is motion:

> I hardly ever think of June 27, 1926
> when I came moaning into my mother's world
> and tried to make it mine immediately
> by screaming, sucking, urinating
> and carrying on generally (291)

Even the dogs O'Hara describes are all characterized by their
actions, except Freckles, who was "boring." The "hazardous
settlement" that is made at the end of poem is "admirable"
because "it moves." Ultimately if anything can be preserved of
the self it will not be some stationary object, like a burial mound,
but some device which moves—the hull of a ship for example:

> I am really an Indian at heart, knowing it is all
> all over but my own ceaseless going, never
> to be just a hill of dreams and flint for someone later
> but a hull laved by the brilliant Celebes response,
> empty of treasure to the explorers who sailed me not (296)

Poets leave behind works that must be reexperienced in time,
that must be "sailed" in order to yield up their treasures again.
In "Ode to Michael Goldberg" references to various kinds of
motion, even to the motion of the poem itself, constitute the main
linking device.

In contrast to the many passages that describe movement and
travelling, there are a number of passages describing stillness.
But it is impossible to stay still, to dwell in any one place for
long:

> I'd like to stay
>   in this field forever
>   and think of nothing

but these sounds,
                    these smells and the tickling grasses
                              "up your ass, Sport"   (291–92)

This is not to say, as "In Memory of My Feelings" says, that each
moment brings a new self. There is a certain necessary attachment to the past which one is always departing from. Childhood,
to which much of this poem is devoted, will always be the origin
of the personality, no matter how unstable or unfixed that personality may be:

    "Je suis las de vivre au pays natal"
        but unhappiness, like Mercury, transfixed me
            there, un repaire de vipères
                and had I known the strength and durability
    of those invisible bonds I would have leaped from rafters onto prongs
                                                            (292–93)

Life is not simply a continuous voyage but a series of
departures from a fixed point of origin, a "sempiternal farewell
to hearths/ and the gods who don't live there" (294). Neither
the meaning of life nor the origin of the personality can be explained merely by looking back: the "gods" are not to be found
beside the hearth. The poet himself must become a kind of god,
joining (at the conclusion of the poem) the "races without time"
and contemplating his life as a timeless whole.
    This sense of timelessness is demonstrated by the structure
of the poem itself. Through O'Hara's transitions (aided by his
periodless, "open" typography) episodes seem to dissolve into
each other. For example, in the following passage a scene from
the poet's childhood in Grafton is gradually transformed into a
scene from his adult life in New York:

when a child
            you wonder if you're not a little crazy, laughing
because a horse
            is standing on your foot
                        and you're kicking his hock
with your sneaker, which is to him
                        a love-tap, baring big teeth
laughing . . .

> thrilling activities which confuse
> >   too many, too loud
> too often, crowds of intimacies and no distance
> >   the various cries
> and rounds
> >   and we are smiling in our confused way, darkly
> in the back alcove
> >   of the Five Spot, devouring chicken-in-the-basket
> and arguing,
> >   the four of us, about loyalty   (296)

A phrase like "crowds of intimacies and no distance" could describe the horse standing on the child's foot, but with the word "crowd" the restaurant scene is underway. During such a passage the poet is not only moving from one incident to another through time, but he is hovering in both temporal periods at once. He is concerned both then and now with the confusion brought about by physical intimacy and love. His consciousness of past and present blends together into an overall consciousness of the self.

"Ode to Michael Goldberg," one of the most humorous and most original autobiographical poems of our era, renders the kind of melange of memories and impressions that undoubtedly spins inside all of us when we try to think about our origins. Threateningly and amusingly, the past moves within us and is part of our self-awareness. The child smelling semen in the hay and hearing the ominous sound of the clattering cutter bar is both the ancestor of, and the same person as, the young man who hears of a sailor's castration by the natives in New Guinea and the adult who conceives of ecstasy as a kind of self-destruction, "contented to be a beautiful fan of blood/ above the earth-empathic earth" (296). To be able to speak eloquently and accurately of this overall consciousness of the self does indeed confer "an extraordinary liberty" upon the imagination.

O'Hara never limits the poem to a mere exploration of sexual anxiety. He binds incidents together not through concepts, but into looser, more suggestive motifs: the "yellow morning" on which the child becomes aware of sex, the "atabrine-dyed hat" of the sailor like a "sick orange sun," and the red of his own blood as he explodes over Palisades Park are part of an over-all color theme (perhaps the "terrible" orange of life itself?) linking these episodes without forcing them into a strictly causal relationship. We are not formed or limited by the past although it is instrumental in exploring our present selves. What O'Hara suggests in this poem is that we retain a provisional knowledge of the past ("things can suddenly be reached, held, dropped and known," 293) which can become part of our rebirth. Because of the past, "a not totally imaginary ascent can begin all over again," but it will inevitably begin, as birth itself began, "in tears."

III   *"Ode on Causality"*

The very different impression made by a work like "Second Avenue" when compared to the poems in *Odes* (1960) can be attributed to the amount of force O'Hara seems to be exerting over his materials. In "Second Avenue," with is unrelenting brilliance of imagery and expression, great force is being expended to hold the elements of the poem as far apart from each other as possible, combatting the natural tendency of thoughts and images to gravitate towards each other and cohere. In later poems, particularly in *Odes,* the meaning of the poem is allowed to come through, but it is not forced through. The poet's mind seems at liberty to be connected or disconnected as it wishes with less fear that a "neurotic coherence" (302) will impose itself. O'Hara's own term for this approach is "keeping the poem open," to allow the poem to shape itself around a whole array of possibilities (554).

It is possible to identify the central thrust of a poem like "Ode to Michael Goldberg" provided we remain undistracted by certain images that may refuse to fall into place. But it is more difficult to do this with the "Ode on Causality," O'Hara's poetic tribute to Jackson Pollock. In *Alone With America* Richard Howard inadvertently renames this poem "Ode on Casualty," which seems a much more appropriate title for a poem whose structure seems so arbitrary and accidental. However, the key to O'Hara's choice of title for this work is that he believed that in certain kinds of artistic creation—in the paintings of Jackson Pollock, and, probably, his own poetry as well—there is no such thing as mere chance. Every gesture the artist makes has an instinctive rightness and order. Accident is then "his strength

and companion" and his work a "denial of accident" (*AC*, 39).
The kind of coherence that O'Hara seems to be striving for is
a chance connection that grows out of the artist's total involvement with the work. (Forced coherence—"suddenly everyone's
supposed to be veined, like marble," 302—leaves the subject
lifeless.) To illustrate this involvement we might think of
Pollock standing physically in the midst of one of his large
canvases, which he insisted on making to the scale of his own
body:

When I am *in* my painting, I'm not aware of what I'm doing. It
is only after a sort of "get acquainted" period that I see what I
have been about. I have no fears about making changes, destroying
the image, etc., because the painting has a life of its own. I try
to let it come through. It is only when I lose contact with the
painting that the result is a mess. Otherwise there is pure
harmony, an easy give and take, and the painting comes out well.
(quoted by O'Hara, *AC*, 39)

The relaxed attitude of the artist to his work is the result of the
deepest kind of involvement with it. Nothing is forced as the
artist allows his work a "life of its own." When at the end of
"Ode to Joy" O'Hara refers to the founding of "great cities where
all life is possible to maintain as long as time" or in "Ode on the
Arrow That Flieth by Day" he refers to the nation "leaning on
the prow" or in "Ode to Willem de Kooning" he speaks of "the
dawn of genius rising from its bed" or in the final lines of "Ode:
Salute to the French Negro Poets" he praises the "poem whose
words become your mouth," O'Hara is celebrating the kind of
human creation that he felt we should "admire/ because it
moves" (298).
    It is with just such an image of creation that O'Hara concludes
the "Ode on Causality." The poem focuses on the enduring
energy of great art, a vitality closely related to the "sexual bliss"
which O'Hara, like Pollock, wishes to "inscribe upon the page of
whatever energy I burn for art. . . ."And it is this energy, more
like a cloud than an inanimate tombstone, that the artist leaves
behind to mark his passing:

. . . reaching for an audience

                    over the pillar of our deaths a cloud

heaves
        pushed, steaming and blasted
                    love-propelled and
                        tangled glitteringly   (303)

But the poem weaves in other thoughts and feelings. As if in rebellion against the very idea of writing an elegy, O'Hara puns on the artistic and sexual meaning of the word "lay." It may be that there is something suspect about the whole notion of being memorialized in poetry—"to be layed at all! romanticized, elaborated, fucked, sung, put to 'rest.'" And isn't there something deadly about elegizing an artist who is in some ways more alive than dead, whose grave does not contain him? The only solution, then, is to write a poem that cannot be contained either. This may explain the ugly, inappropriate frivolity of some of the imagery—i.e., the "Buddhist type caught halfway up/ the tea-rose trellis. . . . " If anything, the poem seems to be turning against its own elegiac intentions, refusing to be totally lyrical or beautiful. "The ugliness we seek in vain/ through life and long for like a mortuarian . . ." is all here in this "tenement of a single heart."

Like the "Ode to Michael Goldberg" this ode has the same impressive, seemingly instinctive network of motifs holding it together against all its wishes to fly off into a whirl of pure energy and motion. The first seven lines, seven seemingly random and detached statements, may well constitute the sort of "get acquainted" period that Pollock speaks of. Once these lines were written, certain motifs were then suggested: stones, bronze, trees, sex, involvement, permanence, art, and the question of coherence and incoherence itself. With the mention of marble, trees and bronze we are led to the scene of Pollock's gravesite and the woods near the cemetery. O'Hara describes "the bronze Jackson Pollock/ gazelling on the rock." (Appropriately, Pollock's name on his tomb is engraved in the energetic calligraphy of his own signature.) But as a child tells him in the opening scene of the poem, Pollock is not under the tomb, "he's out in the woods beyond," and his spirit and the spirit of his art is still alive and moving like the clouds over the cemetery. O'Hara asks Pollock to serve as a guiding spirit for himself, not to watch over his life but to read his work "through copper earth." He wants his own art to have the sexual vitality and the energetic movement of Pollock's: "the thickness in a look of lust, the air within the eye/ the gasp of a moving hand as maps change. . . ."

Nearly all the elements in these images are derived from the opening lines: the "copper" that is in "bronze," the "veined" surface of both the hand and the map, the "look of lust" which recalls the "forms that man has fucked," the "woods" in which Pollock can be found like "one towering tree." And when O'Hara declares that it is "noble to refuse to be added up or divided" he is recalling the opening line in which he speaks of a "sense of neurotic coherence" that the poet may grasp at even though art or life "isn't that simple." The "air within the eye," however, prepares for images to come: the "cloud" of sexual and artistic energy and the "title" that Pollock's art has earned for him: *"Bird in Flight."*

In this way "Ode on Causality" is given an over-all sense of wholeness and coherence. Yet such motifs can hardly include all the images, nor should they. The mood of anguish in this poem is suggested strongly by just those lines and images that seem most inappropriate or "stuck on," like the cigarette butts and old paint tubes encrusted in the surface of one of Pollock's paintings. Just as Pollock insisted that his canvases record his movements, his bloody handprints, his garbage, his own agonized, energetic development, O'Hara, in this poem and so often elsewhere, also seems to be insisting on the right to include the seemingly arbitrary movements of his thoughts above and "beyond any fondness for saying and meaning" (*AC*, 18), and to let the poem stand on its own and be what it is.

IV *"I do this I do that"*

But the "I do this I do that" poems continually assert that such arbitrariness *will* have meaning, that there is no accident if experience is seized with the proper intensity. In examining the construction of the "I do this I do that" poems it should be kept in mind that if there is a form at all it is one that has been allowed to emerge directly from experience and not imposed on experience. Even the emotional thrust of the poem seems to emerge only after a "get acquainted" period in which the poet, by recording what he is doing, finds out how he is feeling:

I better hurry up and finish this
before your 3rd goes off the radio
or I won't know what I'm feeling
                    ("On Rachmaninoff's Birthday #158," 418)

Many times, the mood of the poem is only pinned down at the
very end. In the "I do this I do that" poems O'Hara traces his perceptions, describes his actions, and finally discovers exactly what
he is feeling; and it is this discovery that supplies the connection
for the whole poem.

Often the poem may plunge unexpectedly deeper than the
trivial events described in its opening would ever suggest. "On
Rachmaninoff's Birthday #161," like many poems of this type,
begins with an amusing confession and a setting of the scene:

Diane calls me so I get up
I wash my hair because
I have a hash hangover then
I noticed the marabunta have walked into the kitchen!
they are carrying a little banner
which says "in search of lanolin"
so that's how they found me!

In this passage a bad mood is being concealed behind a façade
of wit. Rather than jumping enthusiastically out of bed, the poet
only gets up because someone has called him. He is not washing
his hair to get clean, but rather to dispel a hash hangover. It is
then that he notices the roaches who seem to him to take the
form of a political procession or crusade. They appear to have
been searching for him (or anyway, for the shampoo). The mis-
guided crusade of the roaches reminds him of the futility of all
human efforts including his own—"there's something wrong with
everyone." This generalization brings the poem a step further
towards whatever it is that the poet is about to define in his
mood. The next two lines build on the seemingly casual, initial
images already established: "Darkness and white hair/ everything empty, nothing there." "Darkness" because the poet has
just gotten up; "white hair" because he has washed his hair, and
has probably discovered a few more white ones; "everything
empty, nothing there" recalls the roaches' futile search for

shampoo in the refrigerator; thus is not a purely metaphysical statement, though it is that, too. The general is emerging from the particular and the mood is defining itself more clearly.

The poet is preoccupied with disturbing thoughts and resigns himself to spending a depressing and boring day: "all day long to sit in a window/ and see nothing but the past." For O'Hara, absorption in the past is a deadening activity which shuts out a full appreciation of life in the present. The mood of the poem is now more clearly defined, and the motif of the meaningless crusade has been further developed. The third section raises this definition of a mood to an eloquent statement about the meaning of such moods. Reminded that he is writing one of his many "On Rachmaninoff's Birthday" poems, he thinks of Russia: "How are things on the stalinallee," he asks, "behind the façades is there despair/ like on 9th street . . ." Despair now seems universal. Political systems are incidental once we penetrate the façade of ideology: the "Cold War" is as pointless as the procession of roaches marching toward the empty refrigerator. But this image of the roaches must be developed one final step further:

> . . . all that life that must be
> struggling on without a silence
> despair is only the first scratch
> of death on the door and a long wait   (419)

The poem now seems to have discovered its center. Melancholy is a premonition of death. Moreover, it is a slow death, "crawling crawling" towards us, a sort of death-in-life. The impact of the poem comes at the very end, at the moment when it discovers its own intention. Images that at first seemed casual take on a suddenly discovered coherence and causality.

When the incidents and thoughts in an "I do this I do that" poem become impossible for O'Hara to fit together, they may ultimately be unified by his acknowledgment of the impossibility of organizing experience:

>   So hot,
> so hot the night my world
>   is trying to send up

its observation satellite.
("Failures of Spring," 274)

At other times the improvisational imagery of the poem may
simply be framed like a jazz composition that begins and ends
with the same theme, so that there may be no clear unity but
at least a return to the point of origin. For example, "Early on
Sunday" begins: "It's eight in the morning/ everyone has left,"
and ends: "Joe stumbles home/ pots and pans crash to the
floor/ everyone's happy again" (404–5).

V *Love Poems and Later Poems*

To a reader searching for coherence, O'Hara's love poems
present few difficulties. It is as if love dominates experience,
unifies perception, and makes "everything," as O'Hara puts it,
"...too comprehensible" (356). Amidst the chaotic details of
a world flooded with incongruous information, the strong emotion of being happy and in love guides both the poet and his
poem towards a definite destination, giving direction and coherence. O'Hara tells his lover in "Sudden Snow":

love is like the path in snow we are making
    though no one else can follow, leading us only
        to the ocean's sure embrace of summer, serious and free
(355)

Although the imagery is in dreamlike disarry we are nevertheless
directed to the poem's essence—the simple idea that love
temporarily sets our anxious lives in order.

In "Sudden Snow" the over-all emotion of being in love seems
to organize an array of seemingly arbitrary details. Love is
defined as motion, and the entire poem, a narrative made up of
non sequiturs and digressions, serves as an example of the
kind of motion that "love is like." The poet calls our attention
to his anxiety about the strange unpredictability of things by
concluding: "you tell me you've got to have eggs for breakfast/
and we divert our course a little without fear." Yet upon closer
analysis certain anxieties have been suggested throughout the
poem. The sudden snow, for example, is a threatening omen.

Inside, at the party, a "company of dancers" is performing, but outside snow is falling and people are slipping. If the snow represents the general law of uncertainty and accident, the path that O'Hara and his lover are "making" that leads them to the "sure embrace of summer" circumvents the dangers of accident, separation and unhappiness.

To waver then, to "divert [one's] course," may mean losing that happiness. But the paradox that O'Hara is exploring is that, despite the accidental nature of experience, his love exists within a certain aura of safety and security. Just as it threatens to teeter—"you look kind of cross"—it rights itself, contrary to the usual law of disaster: "no/ you are proud of my mean tongue." The poet discovers that he can even be loved for what is usually deemed unlikable. Life is full of possibilities: the movies "reach everywhere," the Jehovah's Witnesses print the Bible in all sorts of mellifluous and strange languages, and love follows its own surprising but delightful course. Snow is "quietly and bitterly falling," O'Hara says, "but we don't know that yet." He and his lover are (temporarily, at least) exempt from the usual contingency of the real world.

While "Sudden Snow" may seem bewildering in its copiousness, the theme of love does finally impose some coherence on it. On the other hand, many of the poems that follow the love poems in the 1960's seem to reject any such possbility of order. In these poems O'Hara seems to have returned to the method of "Second Avenue" where coherence would be stifling. It is possible that this increased fragmentation is due to the collapse of tender relationships in O'Hara's life, and the poem that seems to mark this is "A Chardin in Need of Cleaning" (1961):

> What I once wanted is you
> and it is gone . . .
> you were everything once
> > > that
> died of its falsity
> > > and I was
> to blame
> > > but you didn't care
> that something
> > > very beautiful

```
went
        even if it was only an illusion
                        • • • •
                        the (general) (only)
    idea
            is that ideas are bad
                                but what
        if they are kind and generous
                                in a world
    of shits                                    (417)
```

Accompanying the rejection of ideas in his later poetry is the disintegration of those tender illusions of invincibility and joy which infuse so many of his love poems. In such poems "everything is too comprehensible"—indeed, love makes it so—but when love disappears everything becomes too incomprehensible. If ideas are illusions they are at least "kind and generous," but in a state of disillusionment there are no ideas.

Many of the later poems, like "Should We Legalize Abortion," seem confined to a difficult area where public ideas are facile and always wrong, yet private life fails to offer any satisfactory replacements. Beginning with a satire on a public speech about abortion, "Should We Legalize Abortion" finally gives up on the question. There is a moment of acceptance for whatever (serious or trivial) life may bring, however contradictory: "I will always/ go along with therapeutic abortions,/ golf tournaments/ and communion breakfasts." But finally, a haunted ending: "Strange .../ those eyes again!" An attempt to help someone through love fails to produce anything but chaos and disruption:

THERE'S NOBODY AT THE CONTROLS!
                                        Forget
        we ever met.   (482–83)

These later poems often question the meaning of meaningfulness, or, as O'Hara phrases the question: "what of Hart Crane/ what of phonograph records and gin/ what of 'what of'" (387). Though art and culture have previously been the intimate concerns of his life and his poetry, the later poems often seem to dwell on the failure of culture, on the sterility of searching for meaning in art:

why is it that Verdi is closer to us than Aristotle
what difference does it make . . .
my beautiful Cavallon seems to promise something   but
it will never arrive

("Maundy Saturday," 455)

Whereas in a poem like "To the Film Industry in Crisis" the
movies are given one of the most loving tributes they have ever
received in poetry, in a later poem, "Fantasy," it becomes clear
that O'Hara's attachment, or even addiction, to the movies provides him with the simple, orderly values that life itself is no
longer providing: "I'm glad that Canada will remain/ free. Just
free, that's all, never argue with the movies." Moreover, narrative
in the movies affords an almost believable sense of continuity
that life fails to offer: "The main thing is to tell a story./ It
is almost/ very important" (488).

It seems that when O'Hara rejects the values of art, culture,
and especially love, only boredom is left to him. In poems like
"For the Chinese New Year and Bill Berkson" love has disappeared as a meaningful focus of existence: "yes it is strange
that everyone fucks and every-/ one mentions it and it's boring . . ." (391). And this disillusionment with love dissolves
all other values: "it's goodbye/ to lunch to love to evil things
and to the ultimate good as 'well' " (392). In uniform, unpunctuated stanzas, O'Hara explores with a hellish intrepidity
the state of being alive without even being organized enough
to assume a personality. There is only his voice crying "I am a
real human being" as he whirls in the confusion of his disinte-
grating vision: "The strange career of a personality begins at
five and ends/ forty minutes later in a fog" (392). If only a
period would come along, a rest, then at least a sentence would
be completed, establishing something: "it is perhaps the period
that ends/ the problem as a proposition of days of days" (389).
But there can be no definite happiness or clarity in the midst
of this stream of endlessly dissolving moments: "I suppose this
is the happiest moment in infinity" (390), as uncertain as it is,
is about the most positive statement that can be made.

A growing discontent with language as a vehicle of meaning
throws the emphasis in O'Hara's later poetry on the language

itself, particularly on the vernacular "voice," the language of
the moment: "I have something portentous to say to you but
which/ of the papier-mâché languages do you understand" (391).
Whereas in "Second Avenue" a great deal of imagination and
energy were needed to combat the tendency to generalize, and
thus be a poem "about something," in the later poetry many
ideas are included but in the form of bon mots, quips and snatches
of trivial conversation. If, in "Second Avenue," ideas are avoided
in an attempt to write a poem that transcends them, in the later
poetry ideas are often scorned as mere transitory and ephemeral
phenomena and thus recorded as snippets of clever or not-so-
clever talk. These poems communicate an intense restlessness.
There seems to be an increased conviction that if happiness is to
be pursued and located poetry must focus on instants: "god we
were happy for a minute or two" ("F.Y.I."). The poems commemorate moments of happiness that disappear almost as soon
as they are recognized: "The best thing in the world but I
better be quick about it" (Biotherm," 436). There is often a
lost man's recognition that life will be beyond his (or anyone's)
control:

> you find the point of your life
> heading in the wrong direction
> like a compass out of whack, fun!
> because that's the way it goes
> ("F.M.I. 6/25/61," 411)

The poems are full of a restless, desperate search for "fun!"
While the poems in *Odes,* for all their informality, are infused
with a sense of high purpose, a resilient, complex optimism about
the importance of the role of the artist and his art, the later
poems are often infused with O'Hara's boredom and discontent.
The poet is dissatisfied with himself—"I'm so damned literary . . .
I'm so damned empty" (429)—and, what is worse, his poetry also
leaves his intentions unfulfilled:

> . . . alas! this is all I remember of the magnificent poem
>   I made on my walk
>   why are you reading this poem anyway?
>   ("Petit Poème en Prose," 427)

VI   *"Biotherm (For Bill Berkson)"*

O'Hara's difficulty in focusing these later poems may have much to do with the difficulties he was confronting in his life. In "Biotherm," for example, the longest of O'Hara's poems in the 1960's, O'Hara is trying to commemorate his problematic and indefinable relationship with the younger poet, Bill Berkson.[2]

In a key scene in "Biotherm," O'Hara evokes a blend of intimacy and hostility which marks this friendship:

> on the beach we stood on our heads
> I held your legs it was summer and hot
> the Bloody Marys were spilling on our trunks
> but the crocodiles didn't pull them
> it was a charmed life full of
> innuendos and desirable hostilities
> I wish we were back there among the
> irritating grasses and the helmet crabs   (444)

Affection seems to overcome irritation, but crocodiles threatening to pull at their trunks suggests repressed sexual desire and hostility. In "Biotherm" emotion is mocked: "oh god what joy/ you're here/ sob . . ." (442). Even the tenderness between Berkson and O'Hara is played down: "Actually," one says to the other, "I want to hear more about your family," and the other replies, "yes, you get the beer" (446). Replacing tenderness is a private language of giggly in-jokes, and a shared way of looking at the world: "okay, it's not the sun setting it's the moon rising/ I see it that way too" (441).

This private language (and the relationship itself) "is something," O'Hara says, "our friends don't understand" (442). In "Biotherm" O'Hara rejects both love and order: "you were there I was here you were here I was there where are you I miss you/ (that was an example of the 'sonnet' 'form')" (442). Form is mocked because it is related to certain conventions of thought and feeling. Logical relations between certain ideas— "NEVERTHELESS (thank you, Aristotle)" (437)—are seen as belonging to a dead concept of human consciousness, and O'Hara prefers transitions that are more like tiny explosive disappearances: "POOF."

Though it may seem indecipherable on first reading, "Biotherm" is actually rich in seemingly accidental (but often quite interesting) connections. Berkson, for example, is associated throughout the poem with the sky and with the color blue. Sometimes this association is pleasant ("your face/ is like the sky behind the Sherry Netherland/ blue instead of air, touching instead of remote, warm instead of racing," 443) but sometimes it is one of anxiety ("Why do you say you're a bottle and you feed me/ the sky is more blue and it is getting cold," 448). Blue is both the color of sea and sky on sunny days, and also darkness seen through light, a view of chilly depths and infinite space. The ambivalence of the color characterizes O'Hara's attitude toward Berkson: he sees him as both warm and cold, affectionate and "moral" (i.e., sexually reticent).

Many such motifs could be traced. (So many, in fact, that one reader, Marjorie Perloff, perceives "everything in this seemingly wild-talk poem [as being] related to everything else."[3]) And yet they do little to dispel the over-all sense of fragmented disorder and restlessness in the poem. Perhaps the most helpful point of focus for the reader is the predominant tone of "Biotherm"— the careful boundaries of affection and hostility O'Hara maintains. Why would a man make such a poem? If he cannot have love, he can at least have his memories of friendship, his "pretty rose preserved in biotherm" (439), a sunburn preventing salve. Although this relationship fails to offer even the tentative sense of direction that love offers in a poem like "Sudden Snow," it does, at the very least, keep things from "fucking up" (448). Such a relationship, too, deserves to be commemorated. While "For the Chinese New Year" declares with bitter implacability that it is "goodbye/ to lunch to love to evil things and to the ultimate good as 'well'" (392), in "Biotherm" O'Hara at least celebrates lunch, and the milder social pleasures of friendship. Such a fare may seem too crazy a salad for anyone to comprehend, and (though amusing), too limiting and hardly nourishing, but "Biotherm" centers around self-denial after all, not hedonism: "Hear that rattling?" O'Hara asks. "Those aren't marbles in my head they're chains on my ankles" (447). The impatient, short-circuiting rhythm created by the poem's rapid transitions suggests the kind of hobbled, self-constricted movement of a man who finds himself caught up in a relationship in which his feelings cannot simply be allowed to flow. But in "Biotherm" O'Hara is not merely rattling—his very frustration gives this complex poem a coherence of imagery and tone.

CHAPTER 4

The Self

"WHAT is happening to me," O'Hara once wrote, "allowing for lies and exaggerations which I try to avoid, goes into my poems" (500) His overall subject is the flow of his own consciousness, which he tries to render as accurately as he can. Such intentions are large (one man's consciousness might stand for everyone's) but also restricting. If we compare O'Hara briefly to two of his prominent contemporaries who are also personal poets—Allen Ginsberg and Robert Lowell—we can see that his intentions are, on the face of it, much less ambitious.

In Ginsberg's work the poet speaks for (or at least to) the nation, participates in divine revelation, and becomes an agent for moral and political change. Ginsberg's personal wanderings represent a kind of spiritual pilgrimage undertaken by a sometimes bardic, sometimes comic man on behalf of his own and America's enlightenment and salvation. Lowell's life, on the other hand, is the representative life of the troubled man of good intentions who cannot always translate these good intentions into action, and so must regard himself with a measure of guilt. In Lowell's meditations on world history, family history, and personal history, the poet seeks to embody a representative moral vision. In the work of both these poets, social, ethical and spiritual issues are dramatized through the poet's individual experience.

O'Hara was skeptical about such aspirations. He made fun of Lowell's "confessional" mode as a kind of self-aggrandizement through self-accusation: "I think," he said in a 1965 interview with Edward Lucie-Smith, "Lowell has a confessional manner which [lets him] get away with things that are just plain bad but you're supposed to be interested because he's supposed to be so upset" (SS, 13). Towards his close friend, Ginsberg, however, O'Hara's attitude was affectionate but amused. References to Ginsberg in O'Hara's poems reflect O'Hara's doubts about the importance of Ginsberg's spiritual quest: "Allen," said O'Hara in "Adieu to Norman, Bon Jour to Joan and Jean-Paul," "is back talking about God a lot."

Rejecting social and spiritual commitments—wishing to be neither a savior nor a representative sinner—O'Hara focuses completely on his own personal responses. But in doing so he raises a philosophical question: without belief, how is it possible to think of the "self" at all? (Stevens, we recall, referred to "a world in which nothing but the self remains, if that remains.") O'Hara's solution is to think of the self as something that is always in a state of change. By reenacting various movements of the self—from multiplicity to unity, from feeling to detachment, from perception to imagination, from attachment to independence, from self-criticism to self-affirmation—O'Hara's poems become explorations of the movements of consciousness itself. This complex role of the poet in his own poems is a broad theme despite the seeming narrowness of O'Hara's personal focus.

O'Hara's major poem on the self, "In Memory of My Feelings," describes each new feeling giving rise to a new self. These however are eventually rejected. The essential self is constantly sloughing off any new identity as it emerges in order to escape from the trap of self-definition. In addition to moving from self to self, O'Hara also observes himself from multiple perspectives. In "Nocturne" and "Grand Central," for example, he registers his feelings while at the same time observing himself and his situation from the outside as though he were a building. O'Hara also moves in multiple dimensions in his poetry, travelling beyond everyday reality through the imagination. In the "I do this I do that" poems, for example, O'Hara records both his actual movements in the city and his waking dreams as part of the same narrative. In the love poems O'Hara describes his wish *not* to change, not to become a new self, for a new self would put an end to love. And in "Joe's Jacket," one of O'Hara's most fully realized poems, change is described as a form of self-loathing and self-criticism but is ultimately seen as an act of self-affirmation. We will explore more carefully some of these characteristic movements of the self that O'Hara's poems describe. Our main

concern, however, is not to systematize O'Hara's "vision of the
self" into a series of movements, but to determine how the complexity with which O'Hara describes his changing consciousness
makes the subject of his poems larger than the mere events of
his life.

I   Saving the Essential Self: "In Memory of My Feelings"

O'Hara's "In Memory of My Feelings" describes how new
feelings generate new selves. Yet from the midst of the poet's
many selves a vision of an essential self emerges—a self that
is always *becoming* but never is content to be simply what it is,
a self that constantly asserts "I am *not* what I am," and is
determined to escape beyond the boundaries of a fixed personality.

The structure of "In Memory of My Feelings" is complex.
For the moment, though, it will suffice to say that the poem, like
the "Ode to Michael Goldberg," is made up of fragments of
biography and fantasy unified by certain recurring motifs. One
of these, the motif of the serpent, represents the essential self
that must be preserved despite the constant passing away of
one identity after another. In part, O'Hara selects the serpent
as this symbol in order to stress that there is nothing holy about
the self. It is not a soul fashioned by God from pure materials,
which may have become sullied with evil and sin. If anything
the essence of the self lies in its treacherous, lustful, evil impulses,
and from these spring the many "selves" of the poet, like snakes
from the head of the Medusa.

To perceive the self as an array of selves gives the poet great
freedom, even to experiment with the sordid. "I love evil," O'Hara
asserts in "Wind." And in "Poem V(F)W" he tells Vincent
Warren that

> among the relics of postwar hysterical pleasures
> I see my vices
> lying like abandoned works of art
> which I created so eagerly
> to be worldly and modern
> and with it   (347)

Essentially, the self exists as an artist and creator; it has no moral history.

"In Memory of My Feelings" illustrates the poet's freedom to assume various identities, many of them ludicrous, disreputable, sordid. But, most important, the poet exists in a domain where he is free from the onerous consequences of acknowledging a fixed self. The grace O'Hara seeks is, among other things, freedom from worry about grace, the soul, or any of the guilts or responsibilities the traditional self ordinarily assumes:

                                        Grace
to be born and live as variously as possible. The conception
of the masque barely suggests the sordid identifications.
I am a Hittite in love with a horse. I don't know what blood's
in me I feel like an African prince I am a girl walking downstairs
in a red pleated dress with heels I am a champion taking a fall
I am a jockey with a sprained ass-hole I am the light mist
                            in which a face appears
and it is another face of blonde I am a baboon eating a banana
I am a dictator looking at his wife I am a doctor eating a child
and the child's mother smiling I am a Chinaman climbing a mountain
I am a child smelling his father's underwear I am an Indian
sleeping on a scalp
                    and my pony is stamping in the birches,
and I've just caught sight of the *Niña,* the *Pinta* and the *Santa Maria.*
            What land is this, so free?

                                            (256)

This list is the climactic passage in the poem and also, as we shall discover, its point of origin. First, however, we should note that though this list is various and humorously surprising, it is not really as various as possible; it focuses on foreignness, sexuality, and illicitness. The poet is all races—Arab, African, Chinese, Indian—except his own. Moreover, these lines are a celebration of androgyny, as the poet continually changes sexual roles with ease and speed. The jocky with the sprained ass-hole, and the child smelling his father's underwear both suggest sexuality. When he is heterosexual, he is still disreputable: "a dictator looking at his wife." When he is a champion, he is "taking a fall" (i.e. deliberately, having illegally bet against himself). Even as a doctor he eats children, and as a mother he smiles as

the child is being eaten. He is free, that is, to be morally out-
rageous. He arrives in a new land, but not among our historic
explorers; he is already on shore, an Indian "sleeping on a scalp."
It is as though he has discovered a new America in which he is
free to be the savage.

The passage reads like a parody of (and a comic reply to)
Walt Whitman. For Whitman, too, the self is free to become
whatever it observes, no matter how sordid: "I embody," says
Whitman in *Song of Myself,* "all presences outlaw'd or suffering;/
See myself in prison shaped like another man,/ And feel the dull
unintermitted pain."[1] But the difference between O'Hara's use
of the multiple self and Whitman's is that when Whitman takes on
the suffering of another man, his original self remains essentially
clean, unsullied, and healthy. He feels pain the way an angel
would feel pain if he were temporarily given a human body. For
O'Hara, the process of identification is not an act of noble compassion; it is at times playfully wicked (as in the above passage)
and at other times threatening and disorienting:

                                          All
          night I sit on the outspread knees
          of addicts; their kindness
          makes them talk like whores to
          the sun as it moves me hysterically
          forward. The subway shoots onto a ramp
          overlooking the East River, the towers!
          the minarets! The bridge. I'm lost.
                          ("To the Mountains in New York," 199)

In both cases, O'Hara is in a far more confusing state of flux.
Where Whitman's verses are large and leisurely in order to
accomplish one thought, one movement at a time, O'Hara often
intensifies the confusion he describes by cutting the syntax with
enjambments and introducing temporary disorientations: "The
subway shoots onto a ramp..." Where does the ramp lead?
The subway seems to have taken him to Istanbul by mistake.
The East River becomes the Middle East. O'Hara has become
hysterical, whereas Whitman never loses his strength and dignity
to such an extent.

In somewhat the same way that a single musical passage can

generate a symphony, O'Hara composed the poem largely from the material in this list.[2] The "jockey with the sprained asshole," for example, is magnified into an entire racetrack scene in Part 1, and the "child smelling his father's underwear" gives rise to other family passages in Part 2. The "Chinaman climbing a mountain" is developed into a chain of references to climbing and flying. Even images which are left undeveloped and do not generate motifs may connect, however loosely, with other images or references in the poem. If the topics in this list are examined—horses, boats, mountain climbing, family, hunting, politics—we can see that they serve as a core sample of the terrain of the entire work. The boats, for example—the *Niña, Pinta* and *Santa Maria*—connect with various other marine images, the gondola in the opening passage, the German warship *Prinz Eugen,* a "rusted barge/ painted orange against the sea," and so on. One can travel quite confidently through the poem tracing motifs and chains of association.

It is more difficult, however, to determine the poem's meaning objectively. The meaning of the poem must take into account its construction. The poem itself is both multifarious and coherent, provoking the same tension between continuity and disorientation, between identity and multiplicity that O'Hara describes in himself.

From the outset we are warned not to try to reconstruct such a poem in sequential, logical prose. "My quietness," the poem begins, "has a man in it, he is transparent/ and he carries me quietly, like a gondola, through the streets./ He has several likenesses, like stars and years, like numerals." Although we can probably imagine and even comprehend a divided self which is enclosed within attributes of itself like layers of an onion, we must also envision a middle self, the man with "several likenesses." And what are these? Stars and years and numerals. How can a man resemble any or all of these?

What such language does throughout the poem is to draw us within a self which cannot locate or define itself. We can feel, as we read, the "I" of the poem repeatedly branching out. "My transparent selves," we are told at the close of Part 1, "flail about like vipers in a pail, writhing and hissing/ without panic, with a certain justice of response/ and presently the aquiline serpent comes to resemble the Medusa." As in the opening passage, the self is not further defined by such language, but fragmented. One of the poet's selves comes to resemble himself (it even has O'Hara's "aquiline" nose), but that self, in turn, resembles the female Medusa whose head bristles with serpents. Thus, out of the self that resembles O'Hara come other serpents (and other selves?). The poem is full of images of multiplicity that lead to renewed multiplicity.

At the end of the poem, however, a single serpent (and a single self) seems to emerge:

> And now it is the serpent's turn.
> I am not quite you, but almost, the opposite of visionary.
> You are coiled around the central figure,
>   the heart
> that bubbles with red ghosts, since to move is to love
> and the scrutiny of all things is syllogistic,
> the startled eyes of the dikdik, the bush full of white flags
> fleeing a hunter,
>   which is our democracy. . . .   (256)

A visionary imagines an ideal and may even try to attain it, but O'Hara is always avoiding what he imagines he might become. The instant an image of the self emerges, O'Hara moves away from it. Yet the "central figure" is still the heart which is haunted by "ghosts" of past loves. As inevitable as the desire to change is the desire to love, and yet, O'Hara declares, it is necessary for him to deduce his position in the world from his circumstances. He must respect only what these circumstances tell him he *is*, not what he wishes to be.

And in scrutinizing what he is, his chief desire is to be something else. It is worth noticing the restless multiplicity of the language here—the serpent comes from the domain of religious myth; "visionary" and "syllogistic" from the language of philosophy; "the central figure" from art criticism; "bubbles with red ghosts" from fantasy; the "dikdik" (a small antelope) from zoology; the "white flags" from the vocabulary of warfare; "our democracy" from the rhetoric of politics. The essential self that emerges may be singular but it always has the potential for limitless multiplicity, and will continue to generate new feelings and new selves in the future.

The poet cannot be a historian of these selves (a historian's vision is far more tranquil and orderly); he can, however, take pieces of his personal history and put them into his poems:

> I went to Chicago,
> an eventful trip: the fountains! the Art Institute, the Y
> for both sexes, absent Christianity.
> At 7, before Jane
> was up, the copper lake stirred against the sides
> of a Norwegian freighter.... (255)

Such fragments of autobiography can be made to fit into the overall texture of this multifarious but well-knit poem by subtly highlighting and adjusting the colorations of the language. The "Y for both sexes" connects with the images of transsexuality in the list passage quoted above. "Absent Christianity" suggests the serpent; there is even something faintly serpentine in the image of the stirring "copper lake." The proper use of an autobiographical fragment, O'Hara is telling us, is as a tile to be fitted into the overall mosaic of the poem. The history of the self has no importance or validity in itself, but only as one of various kinds of materials that can be used in a poem. To rescue the essential self the poet makes works of art.

"I have lost," the poet tells us at the end, "what is always and everywhere/ present, the scene of my selves, the occasion of these ruses,/ which I myself and singly must now kill/ and save the serpent in their midst." As the title suggests, the poet's feelings have died and he is "memorializing" them. And yet, he expresses himself paradoxically. How can he have "lost" something that is "always and everywhere/ present"? And why should he have to "kill" what he has already "lost"? In a process that is never finished, the poet writes poems to define his feelings and to abolish them as definitions of himself. The single, essential self that emerges at the end of the poem is the unfaithful, constantly self-betraying serpent shedding selves like skins. The serpent-self, O'Hara is saying, is the ideal self of the artist: faithful to nothing except the need to change—which is also, inevitably, the need to create anew.

II *Observing the Self*

Throughout O'Hara's work the self is constantly changing in response to feeling. But poems cannot merely be simple expressions of emotion—news reports on the poet's internal life—because O'Hara is well aware that reporting on feelings falsifies them. For this reason he externally observes the self as a kind of independent construction. He can, in this way, dramatize his feelings but also present them with humor and an ironic perspective that expels them from himself. This is what I am feeling, the poems seem to be saying, and yet I am also somewhere else, somewhere outside of these feelings. The essential self of the artist stands apart and scrutinizes his emotional life as a kind of spectacle. O'Hara watches the extravagant performance of his own emotions, often imagining bizarre transformations. In "To the Harbormaster" the poet describes himself as a ship

> In storms and
> at sunset, with the metallic coils of the tide
> around my fathomless arms. . . .   (217)

In "Ode" he writes:

> I become the sea—
> in love with your speed, your heaviness and breath.   (196)

In "Life on Earth" he becomes a bell:

In the darkness I am growing larger!
In the darkness I am growing louder!
I am swinging and clanging inside myself like the tongue of a bell!
> (157)

While in "Bill's Burnoose," "O the dark!/ I the TV!"

O'Hara writes with intensity, but exhibits a sense of detachment in viewing his own emotional transformations. In "Nocturne," a simple but charming poem about lost love, and in "Grand Central," a more intense and complex poem about sexual repression and frustration, O'Hara uses the technique of projecting himself into other shapes—in both cases, well-known

New York buildings. But in these poems also the poet's feelings are accompanied by his own detached perspective on himself.

"Nocturne" provides a clear illustration of this technique. O'Hara begins with a straightforward appeal for sympathy from his beloved: "There's nothing worse/ than feeling bad and not/ being able to tell you." O'Hara's remedy is to avoid self-pity and transform himself into some object that will resemble his feelings so that they can be understood from a more distant and removed perspective—in this case, the United Nations Building:

> My eyes, like millions of
> glassy squares, merely reflect.
> Everything sees through me,
> in the daytime I'm too hot
> and at night I freeze; I'm
> built the wrong way for the
> river and a mild gale would
> break every fiber in me.
> Why don't I go east and west
> instead of north and south?
> It's the architect's fault.
> And in a few years I'll be
> useless, not even an office
> building.

The appeal for sympathy, the self-pity, has been redirected onto the U.N. Building. It too, after all, hopes for some kind of union, but is passively locked to one location, cannot travel, and is doomed to uselessness because of its faulty design. The feeling of being exposed, passive and helpless in confronting the space between himself and another is subtly expressed. The poem is visual like the building—it merely reflects—and because the lover is absent, the words to describe exactly in what way the speaker is "feeling bad" are also absent. Indeed, the possibility for any coherent message to anyone evaporates, and "Nocturne" simply ends with a list of perceptions:

> Because you have
> no telephone, and live so

> far away; the Pepsi-Cola sign,
> the seagulls and the noise.   (225)

The poet, like a building that is all windows, is looking out
rather than in, and not directly speaking his complaint. The
gigantic metaphor he erects to represent himself and his feelings does, however, like the Pepsi-Cola sign, get the "message"
through, but it is rendered more complex because of O'Hara's
external perspective.

It is not the poet who allows himself to voice the trite complaints that "it's the architect's fault" and "in a few years I'll
be useless." It is the snobbish, self-pitying U. N. Building
speaking here. In a parody of his own desire to complain, O'Hara
sees himself in the guise of a building complaining about all the
immutable facts of its existence. This self-parody effectively
removes O'Hara's feelings to some point outside himself so that
he can objectively and humorously examine them.

"Grand Central," a more troubling and intense poem, deals
with psychic pain. The poet sees himself as a railroad terminal
which contains an enormous amount of energy but is unable
to move at all. Reversing Walt Whitman's heroic stance, O'Hara
represses his tremendous sexual drive. He instead appears passive,
corpselike, enduring the agony resulting from sexual frustration.
His alternative is to imitate the action of "a friend" who

> took a letter carrier across
> the catwalk underneath the dome. . . .
> He unzipped the messenger's trousers
> and relieved him of his missile. . . .   (169)

This anecdote—told breathlessly and in detail—enables us to
feel the poet's temptation, as well as his revulsion and renun-
ciation. The terminal becomes his "cathedral" because of the
suffering that he has undergone. Self-humiliation may be "one
way of dominating the terminal," but the poet has not resorted
to it; humiliating acts can be tantamount to suicide (the mes-
senger's penis is a "smoking muzzle") but O'Hara would prefer
to dominate through a more active and self-affirming passion
and violence. Like Tolstoy's Anna Karenina, he can turn a
stifled and repressed life into a fatal victory.

"Grand Central" is both agonized and satirically witty. The passage about the "enormous bullets" that bury themselves in the poet's body comes dangerously close to what might be called O'Hara's superman mode. (This can be seen much more blatantly, however, in "Poem (I am not sure there is a cure)": "Clouds! Do you see this fist?/ I have just put it through you!/ Sun! you do well to crouch/ and snarl, I have willed you away.") Yet it is tempered with humor. "Grand Central" oscillates through degrees of seriousness. At one extreme, the ending advances the idea of victimization as a way of "dominating." At the other extreme, the central section strays off into fantasy and satire. The trains, O'Hara tells us, are on their way "to some devastated island/ where they will eat waffles with the/ other Americans of American persuasion." O'Hara has a body that he ridicules as an anonymous Renaissance-style structure, like Grand Central Station in New York. "It is riddled with bullets, am I," says O'Hara; the bullets are clearly instances of pain, but his tone is detached, as he wavers between seeing himself as "it" and as "I."

Surveying the spectacle of himself as "an expanse of marble floor/ covered with commuters and information," O'Hara fashions a sepulchral monument out of his own body, pities it, worships it, and, at the same time, is amused about it all. This blend of amusement and agony conveys, ultimately, an attitude of acceptance and courage. Though O'Hara has a number of amusing poems about homosexuality, "Grand Central" is his strongest poem on homosexual frustration and conflict. It is convincing precisely because the poet participates in his own suffering and observes it at the same time.

III Combining the Waking Self and the Dreaming Self

Another way that O'Hara steps outside of himself is through dream-fantasy. Though the poet cannot achieve a historical perspective, this need not mean that the self is confined to the present moment alone. The poet can transcend time through the imagination. O'Hara's poems are frequently biographical and factual, but they are also imaginative. Though private experience cannot be emblematic of moral truth, or lead to prophetic revelation, it need not be completely mundane. The self moves through the waking world, but it also moves through the world of dreams and fantasy—a world which is outside of time.

We can see this most clearly in what appear to be O'Hara's most factual, biographical works: his "I do this I do that" poems. In these the New York scene is blended with dream imagery so that reality somehow takes on the inexplicable strangeness and arbitrariness of a dream.

In "A Warm Day for December," for example, O'Hara creates the sense of walking down Fifty-seventh Street and at the same time the sense of walking in the air down Fifty-seventh Street. The poem contains both real events—"meeting Roy and Bill I drink Vermouth"—and imaginative transformations:

> I am a microcosm in your macrocosm
> and then a macrocosm in your microcosm
> a hydrogen bomb too tiny
> to make an eye water   (375–76)

At times the poet is lost in the vast world, and at other times his consciousness dwarfs the world, a vast power confined to a tiny space. "I am in the air/ yet I follow 57th"—the real world, 57th Street, is "almost there" but transformed by the power of the poet's private world—his spaceship-phonebooth. At the same time that he is separated from the people walking by the glass walls of the phonebooth, he is also intimately in touch with the person with whom he is speaking on the phone. The ecstatic feeling of being in love with this person, in turn, makes him feel that he *is* the people walking by: "then I open the door the sounds rush over me the people." The comma that should separate him from "the people" is missing, and actions drift into each other in a dreamy, unpunctuated flow.

Even when fantasy plays less of a role, and the poem seems to be more literally descriptive, the city world is still being transformed by the poet's imagination and feelings. In "A Step Away From Them," the real details of a walk around the city are selected and arranged in such a way that they take on the arbitrariness of a dream. The poem begins: "It's my lunch hour, so I go/ for a walk . . . ." There is no reason for the walk, no destination—it is simply lunch time. The "I" in this poem is naive. He is not certain why construction workers wear yellow

helmets—"They protect them from falling/ bricks, I guess"—
and he used to think the Armory Show took place in the Manhattan Storage Warehouse. As is so often the case in O'Hara's
poetry, the poem is full of real details which seem surreal: "On/
to Times Square, where the sign/ blows smoke over my head,
and higher/ the waterfall pours lightly." And the street world
behaves like a strange mechanism whose causal relationships
are not clear:

> A blonde chorus girl clicks: he
> smiles and rubs his chin. Everything
> suddenly honks: it is 12:40 of
> a Thursday.

It is as if the honking is somehow triggered by the man rubbing
his chin, a gesture triggered in turn by the clicking of the chorus
girl. The poem creates the mood of being lost and feeling strange
among the most familiar details of the New York scene—a kind
of incipient Surrealism. Even the way the lines are arranged
creates this effect:

> glistening torsos sandwiches
> and Coca-Cola, with yellow helmets.   (257)

The enjambments break up the logic of the syntax, the familiar
arrangement of things, and give us sandwiches made of torsos
and Coco-Cola bottles capped with yellow helmets.

As in "A Warm Day for December," the technique here is
to create a dual atmosphere of reality and surreality. The world
of dreams and the waking world coexist, just as the self of the
poet is split: eyes, ears, feet and mind are walking on the street,
but his heart is elsewhere, it is in his pocket and has become a
book of poems by Pierre Reverdy, a Surrealist poet, but also one
who likes to list images of things seen. Because he wishes to be
both involved in his feelings and detached from them—to be
able to overcome emergencies by "re-emerging" in the guise of
another self—O'Hara often adopts the outmoded convention of
thinking of the heart as an organ of feeling and emotion, rather
than merely a pump. Throughout his poetry he frequently refers
to his heart as leading a separate existence from the rest of his

body and his mind: "I am sobbing, walking on my heart" (195),
"That's no furnace, that's my heart" (194), "... my// petulant
two-fisted heart" (78). In "A Step Away from Them," just as in
other "I do this I do that" poems like "The Day Lady Died" and
"Personal Poem," the theme is absent-heartedness. The sunlit
world of the New York streets is somehow not the only reality
because the poet's heart is with people who are absent or dead.
Perhaps it is their absence that gives the world a slightly
strange, unfamiliar appearance, and makes O'Hara feel displaced.
While he recognizes that he is living in the transitory realm of
clock time—"I look/ at bargains in wristwatches ... it is 12:40
of/ a Thursday"—he prefers to take refuge in the timeless world
of art. Unlike the Manhattan Storage Warehouse, "which they'll
soon tear down," poetry creates an indestructible warehouse
where O'Hara's heart takes refuge.

In his "I do this I do that" poems, O'Hara traces his everyday activities while surveying the spectacle of his own inner
life. When he fails to do this, the result can be flat and uninteresting:

It is 4:19 in Pennsylvania Station
and we are running to catch the train for East Hampton
strange train! for it will take us to Patsy and Mike
and how can it? (since we love them and are there)
but we go, because of seeing (how important it is)
and Maxine (why are you here? because of Larry? yes)
and Mary, sweetie, it was lovely having drinks at your studio
and I, for five, enjoyed dinner although nobody else seemed to
because of the portrait of Mamma Lanza   (PR, 184)

This poem, beginning with a statement of the time, and concerning an upcoming train trip to the Hamptons, is reminiscent
of the opening of O'Hara's greatest "I do this I do that" poem,
"The Day Lady Died," written about a month later. But "It is
4:19 in Pennsylvania Station" is merely factual, not internal or
imaginative (except for a faint glimmer in line four where O'Hara
touches on the theme of absence and timelessness). When O'Hara
succeeds in merging his actual, outer life with his inner imaginative life, he succeeds in rendering an image of the self that
has all the complexity of actual mental and physical motion—a

record of moving *and* being moved. But he is doing more than recording his feelings of the moment. He is also writing about the self as it exists apart from the present moment, a self both involved in daily life and haunted by "ghosts" of the past.

IV *Opposing the Self That Changes with the Self That Loves*

For O'Hara the essential self derives its survivor's strength from constant transformation, but this power to change, to move on to the next moment reborn, is threatened by love. As O'Hara says to his beloved in "Les Luths," "the clock ... will not make me know how to leave you" (343). Although O'Hara has mastered "the speed and strength which is the armor of the world" (217), it is love that threatens to slow him down and make him regret change.

In O'Hara's poetry, love for others constitutes a major assault against the self:

for six seconds of your beautiful face I will sell the hotel and commit
an uninteresting suicide in Louisiana where it will take them
                              a long time
to know who I am/ why I came there/ what and why I am and
                        made to happen   (351)

Here, at the end of "Hotel Transylvanie," O'Hara is evoking l'Abbé Prévost's tragic love story of the Chevalier Des Grieux and Manon Lescaut. For Des Grieux, love is "what and why I am and made to happen"; it both debases his life and gives it purpose. O'Hara seems to find Des Grieux's situation emblematic of the lover's situation in general: the self is assaulted and forged by emotions (especially love) that the world provokes in us. We become what we love, and our identity is reshaped by our feelings. But this identity cannot remain fixed.

Love, then, for O'Hara, as he suggests with *Love Poems* (*Tentative Title*), is at best a tentative connection. A lasting and permanent love requires a lasting and consistent self, and yet, for O'Hara, the effect of falling in love is that the self becomes changed. Many of O'Hara's love poems are about the impossibility of permanent love, and begin with an awareness of "the/ endless originality of human loss" (331). In "Ballad" O'Hara

asks "why is it that I am alway separated from the one I love"
and immediately concludes: "it is because of/ some final thing"
(368).

The desire to appropriate someone by loving him is seen as
a kind of "tampering." In this beautiful poem there are only two
images, and both of these images—that of a potted palm, and
that of a ferry transforming itself into a bicycle—are images of
tampering with another's and finally with one's own identity.

To love, then, we must both change or "transplant" the beloved and change ourselves. But in doing this (or in trying to do
it) love is destroyed because both people have ceased to be
themselves. The "final thing" that makes love impossible is the
movement of life itself, the constant fluctuation of the self. Love
can only take place

> where nothing happened
> and we both were simply that
> and we loved each other so
> and it was so unusual   (368)

Love, as O'Hara sees it, is a special moment of stillness temporarily exempt from time and change.

O'Hara's poems about love tend to circle around the concepts
of presence and absence, permanence and change. In "Those Who
Are Dreaming, A Play About St. Paul," O'Hara doubts the existence of permanent love and views the love that endures even
when the beloved is physically absent as a mere powerless abstraction. This abstraction, like the dread "mechanism" of the
telephone which brings him only his lover's "voice" is at best
only a flimsy protection against the threat of losing this love.
"Those Who Are Dreaming" is a poem about the temporary joy
of assuming an identity: answering the telephone the poet "says
hello/ this is George Gordon, Lord Byron." It is also about the
imminent loss of identity when the beloved is absent:

> . . . as one continues
> to try to make something appear between divided selves
> clear and abstract as the word *thing* preceded by
> another word, so you have lingered.   (374)

The poignancy of the poem originates precisely in that final verb. Whatever lingers is not lasting but is on the verge of disappearing. Between the "divided selves" of the poet and his lover it is impossible to created something lasting, just as it is impossible for the poet to remain long in one identity without sacrificing his essential self.

Other poems by O'Hara depict love as adding a new significance, a new warmth to the present moment, and thus providing a reality that transcends time and space:

> though a block away you feel distant the mere presence
> changes everything like a chemical dropped on a paper
> and all thoughts disappear in a strange quiet excitement
> I am sure of nothing but this, intensified by breathing
> ("Poem [Light clarity avocado salad in the morning]," 350)

Love can serve as an amulet protecting the poet from the emptiness of being alive only in the present: "love is love nothing can ever go wrong/ though things can get irritating boring and dispensable." But the test for the efficacy of love is still its power to infuse the present moment with a "strange quiet excitement." Love does not invest our lives with an absolute sense of values, but only serves to color the present. Romantic love influences the mood of the moment; it infuses it with false but delightful feelings of permanence and invincibility:

> when I am in your presence I feel life is strong
> and will defeat all its enemies ...
>   ... once we are
> together we always will be in this life come what may
> ("Poem À la recherche d' Gertrude Stein," 349)

But the exaggerated absolutes indicate O'Hara knows all too well that this cannot be so, as much as he may wish it.

V *Affirming the Self as it Changes: "Joe's Jacket"*

Even stronger than the desire to love, in O'Hara's view, is the desire to change. Since the self exists apart from moral judgments, such change does not necessarily mean improvement. But O'Hara sees the desire to change as part of an overall desire

to live. In "Joe's Jacket" O'Hara describes the flow of his own
life and feeling, and in doing so illustrates the process of self-
transformation that ensures the survival of the essential self.

"Joe's Jacket" is O'Hara's most complete effort at self-
portraiture. Somewhat the way a man may have a picture taken
of himself before getting married, or before setting out on a
long voyage, O'Hara records for us his own motions, thoughts
and feelings over the span of an entire weekend (the longest
period of time in any of O'Hara's "I do this I do that" poems)
during which he first fell in love with Vincent Warren.[3] The poem
contains within it a meditation on the limitations of self-expression. Honesty, in O'Hara's milieu, is an obligatory tactic
to assure friends of one's affection; indeed, since being honest is
the most difficult of poses (as Oscar Wilde tells us), O'Hara
wonders whether it is even worth the trouble. Going further
than Oscar Wilde's comic cynicism, O'Hara denies that honesty
is possible even in his revealing conversations with *himself*.

The refrain of the poem "now I will say it, thank god, I
knew you would," conveys precisely the tone of O'Hara's self-
revelations. The first time this line is uttered it sums up the
attitude O'Hara's group of friends have toward confession. In
discussing their feelings for each other O'Hara notices that his
friends deflect their expressions of affection into an excitable
sharing of confidences—confidences that are not quite so honest,
or at least not quite so earthshaking, as both teller and listener
like to pretend.

The second time the line is used it refers to O'Hara's confession concerning his drinking:

I drink to smother my sensitivity for a while so I won't stare away
I drink to kill the fear of boredom, the mounting panic of it
I drink to reduce my seriousness so a certain spurious charm
can appear and win its flickering little victory over noise
I drink to die a little and increase the contrast of this
                              questionable moment
and then I am going home, purged of everything
    except anxiety and self-distrust
now I will say it, thank god, I knew you would
and the rain has commenced its delicate lament over the orchards
                                                          (330)

Few moments in O'Hara's poetry are quite this naked. His self-estimate is witty, imaginative and precise. The line he used satirically in describing his friends' manner of confessing to each other he now uses to describe himself. Yet even this moment of nakedness between the poet and himself is accompanied by a certain "self-distrust." Backing away from the pride inherent even in such articulate self-loathing, O'Hara connects it first to the confessional games his friends play with each other, and then to the rain's "lament," something self-nourishing and self-worshipping in nature which suggests the poet's fear of narcissim. Through irony and self-scrutiny he "kills off" the feelings he confesses, and destroys even this insightful self-definition as being somehow spurious. He is ready now to assume a new sense of self.

The image of rain lamenting over the orchard introduces the scene of O'Hara lying in bed in the morning reading D. H. Lawrence's "Ship of Death," a poem which begins: "Now it is autumn and the falling fruit/ and the long journey towards oblivion.// The apples falling like great drops of dew/ to bruise themselves an exit from themselves."[4] In Lawrence's serene and beautiful poem the self dies, sails into a kind of oblivion and is reborn. The death journey that Lawrence describes, the soul sailing with its "little ship," is actual death, and the rebirth at the end is Lawrence's rendering of resurrection and reincarnation. In the flow of life and incident that O'Hara is rendering, however, the self (without dying) is reborn between the reading of one book and another during an ordinary weekend in Southampton:

an enormous window morning and the wind, the beautiful des-
                    peration of a tree
fighting off strangulation, and my bed has an ugly calm
I reach to the D.H. Lawrence on the floor and read "The Ship
                    of Death"
I lie back again and begin slowly to drift and then to sink
a somnolent envy of inertia makes me rise naked and go to the window
where the car horn mysteriously starts to honk, no one is there
and Kenneth comes out and stops it in the soft green lightless stare
and we are soon in the Paris of Kenneth's libretto, I did not drift
away I did not die I am there with Haussmann and the rue de Rivoli

and the spirits of beauty, art and progress, pertinent and mobile
in their worldly way, and musical and strange the sun comes out
                                                                    (330)

The trumpet of the last judgment announcing his rebirth is a car
horn that goes off accidentally, and O'Hara plunges into the
world of Kenneth's libretto. He has moved from Lawrence's
otherworldly poem to Koch's worldly opera about the redesigning
of Paris, and the sun obliges by coming out "musical and strange."
It is as if, once again, the shift of mood is mysteriously in harmony
with the weather, the rain of last night's "lament" giving way to
the sun of today's reawakening.

As O'Hara returns to Manhattan by car, his and Vincent
Warren's "forceful histories . . . loom/ like the city hour after
hour closer and closer to the future" until O'Hara gets home to
his apartment and his roommate Joe LeSueur. They do not talk
things over at all, but, in contrast to the incessant confidences
exchanged by friends in Southampton, and even to the self-reveal-
ing confessions O'Hara made to himself, he and Joe talk "only
of the immediate present and its indiscriminately hitched-to-
past." It is a kind of directionless conversation which, because it
feels no need to focus on what is most important, is willing to
take in everything. This provokes in O'Hara the feeling that
life in his beloved city is "bathed in an unobtrusive light which
lends things/ coherence and an absolute, for just that time as
four o'clock goes by." Unlike the light from his "Barbizonian
kiddy days," to which he refers in the first stanza, this is no
longer a landscape "lit from above" like a painting in the manner
of the school of Barbizon (all light derived from one divine
source giving everything coherence), nor is it the "soft green
lightless stare" of predawn, when the self is molting, but it
is a light coming from everywhere whose source is in all the
things it illuminates. The world is its own source of grace; each
moment provides its own "coherence," its own "absolute."

Joe's jacket, which O'Hara borrows later that morning to wear
to work, symbolizes the protective continuity of O'Hara's longstanding relationship with LeSueur:

when I last borrowed it I was leaving there it was on my
                    Spanish plaza back

and hid my shoulders from San Marco's pigeons was jostled on
the Kurfürstendamm
and sat opposite Ashes in an enormous leather chair in the Continental
it is all enormity and life it has protected me and kept me here on
many occasions as a symbol does when the heart is full and
risks no speech
a precaution I loathe as the pheasant loathes the season and
is preserved
it will not be need, it will be just what it is and just what happens
(330)

But what is also being conveyed here is the rejection of the
"precaution" of self-definition and the liberation of the essential
self which will always seek to remain free of definition: "it will
be just what it is." O'Hara, with the same precision that dis-
tinguished his earlier passage on his drinking, defines his feeling
towards himself clinging to the good luck charm of Joe's jacket
(and to the reliable and consistent friendship) even while he
loathes such an attitude. Symbols imply a fixed universe with
knowable relations, but, as he always has, O'Hara now affirms
his acceptance of change and fluidity. His self-loathing this time
results not in self-satire but in an instantaneous resolution to
welcome whatever happens, to function not according to "need"
but in the spirit of adventure and continual rebirth. This lightning shift of tone and attitude—from a fancy, hunted bird who
"loathes" the precaution of the season and is "preserved," to
the simple, brave, almost entirely monosyllabic affirmation in
the last line—jolts us out of the usual lyrical and symbolic
language of poetry into the simplest possible speech, the mind
directing instructions to itself. Without the need to refer to
the symbols of death and resurrection or reincarnation, letting
the rapid, merging, periodless grammar and the fast narrative
pace of the poem come to stand for what it is, for fluidity itself,
O'Hara enables us to feel the self-affirming change during the
split second when the self changes.

In a world where there may be nothing larger than man to
believe in—"what/ can heaven mean up, down, or sidewise," as
O'Hara says in "For Bob Rauschenberg"—O'Hara's poems affirm
the significance of the individual life at every moment, dark,
light, and inbetween. "The frail instant needs us," he says to his

artist friend, not necessarily to make order out of it, or to transform it into an eternal truth, but simply to celebrate it with deep attention. By denying a fixed self, and affirming instead the self that is always becoming, O'Hara is able to focus on the momentary without being false to the ever-changing, provisional quality of self-awareness and human feeling:

> what has happened and is here, a
> paper rubbed against the heart
> and still too moist to be framed.   (322)

CHAPTER 5

Feelings

And I see in the flashes
what you have clearly said,
that feelings are our facts.
As yet in me unmade.
                    "To Edwin Denby"

O'HARA claimed in his 1965 interview with Edward Lucie-
Smith to have arrived at a simple standard for excellence
in his own poetry—truth. Asked how to distinguish truth he replied
that a poem was true when

> you don't find that someone is making themselves more elegant,
> more stupid, more appealing, more affectionate or more sincere than
> the words will allow them to be. . . . I can see it when I reread
> some of my poems that I went overboard and that the words are
> showing quite clearly to anyone who's bothered to look at them
> closely enough: that it's bullshit, you know. And that's what I
> don't like.   (SS, 14)

Described in this way, the language of poetry serves as a kind of
truth test. Indeed, as O'Hara suggests here, it is no longer
enough for the reader to be convinced that the poet is sincere.
The key question is one of self-consciousness. Is the poet aware
that by expressing his feelings he is falsifying them? Feelings
may be facts, but only as long as they remain undefined. The
emotional truth O'Hara is striving for contains within itself
its own denial. Just as the self in O'Hara's poetry seems to declare "I am not what I am," so too O'Hara's poems constantly
suggest "I am not feeling (only) (exactly) what I am feeling."
     Occasionally, as O'Hara himself suggests, passages in his
work "go overboard" and fail to convey this kind of self-aware-

113

ness. In the love poem "[The Light Comes On By Itself]," the refrain "*I am waiting for you to love me*" is used to suggest that
while the poet's mind may be perceiving his surroundings and the
changes taking place, his body has only one contant desire which
it repeats with every breath. But why should the body be so
much more uncomplicated than the mind? O'Hara seems to be
taking his feelings, his own desire for love, too seriously and one-
dimensionally, and the refrain is unlike his usual alert, self-scruti-
nizing idiom. Yet such instances of outright emotional over-
simplification are rare in O'Hara's work. He hardly ever at-
tempts to be "more sincere" than his own language permits, and
this conveys a sense of emotional authenticity that is one of his
work's most valuable qualities.

This chapter will concentrate on O'Hara's feelings about
death, friendship and love—three frequent topics in his poetry.
In his poems on death, O'Hara believes that it is wrong to try
to sum up his reactions too neatly. Some of his most interesting
elegies are antielegies—poems about the impossibility of writing
an adequate elegy. In such poems—we will focus on "Four Little
Elegies" as an example—various changes and complexities of
voice signal the poet's desire to undercut any tendency to over-
simplify and memorialize the dead. But in O'Hara's best poem
on death, "The Day Lady Died," an offhand, digressive, delaying
manner contributes to the intensity of the elegiac mood at the
end.

In his poems about friendship, O'Hara often complicates the
feelings he expresses by making us aware of the occasions on
which they are being offered. In "Poem Read At Joan Mitchell's,"
for example, a public tribute to two friends about to marry,
we sense beneath his overt affection a subtle countercurrent of
anxiety and estrangement. Yet the act of writing the poem
demonstrates O'Hara's true friendship for these people, despite
his mixed feelings.

In the love poems, O'Hara's usual irony (expressed through
interruption and contradiction) is less evident. These are
"delicate and caressing poems," written from his "naked heart"
(356). The poet is aware that time itself will undermine his
feelings of love, so he need not do it himself. Throughout the
love poems to Vincent Warren, O'Hara expresses his awareness
of the ephemeral fragility of love in images of light and dark-

ness. These poems are a narrative of changing feelings during the course of a love affair and as a sequence have a complexity that many of the individual poems lack.

I *Death*

A poet, in O'Hara's view, has to "deal with" sentiment as bravely as possible: "You're sort of galloping into the midst of a subject," he told Lucie-Smith, "and just learning about you, you know. You're not afraid to think about anything and you're not afraid of being stupid and you're not afraid of being sentimental. You just sort of gallop right in and deal with it" (SS, 25). But the subject of death seems to have been a difficult one for O'Hara to manage. In his elegies he deliberately undercuts his own expressions of grief with a highly self-conscious verbal surface. In several of them, the poet interrupts himself, beginning again in a new voice, a though trying to prevent the poem from straying into falseness.

The best way to guard against falsification of feeling may well be to avoid uttering it, to interrupt, break the tone, disturb the too-easy flow of the poem. In "The 'Unfinished'," O'Hara's poem about why he could not write a suitable elegy for his close friend, Bunny Lang,[1] he changes voice in just this way: "The casual reader," O'Hara says, "will not I am sure, be averse to a short/ digression in this splendid narrative." He then goes on to tell a brief, tongue-in-cheek parable about "a person who one day in a fit of idleness decides to make/ a pomander like the one that granny used to have around the/ house in old New England. . . ." This pomander stands for the ill-advised desire to enshrine and preserve one's emotions, particularly one's grief. The orange is killed by the cloves that are supposed to preserve it: "That's/ what you get, baby," says O'Hara. He means that by taking something living, something in process, something unfinished and turning it into a product or history, the result is more than likely to be false and dead. O'Hara was afraid his elegies would erase his living memory of friends who died.

For this reason, his best elegies are for public figures rather than for friends. But how seriously does O'Hara take such elegies? For example, he wrote four elegies for James Dean.[2] In the best of them, O'Hara's beautiful and funny series-poem,

"Four Little Elegies," his seriousness is questionable, and it is this up-in-the-air quality that makes it so suitable for its subject— a movie idol, dead at age twenty-four.

In the final section, O'Hara actually assumes the voice of Dean. In doing so he risks sentimental excess. But we would be misinterpreting O'Hara if we assumed, as A. Poulin, Jr. does in his essay "Contemporary American Poetry: The Radical Tradition," that because O'Hara wrote about singers and movie stars the poems suggest "the emptiness, if not the decadence of the emotion."[3] On the contrary, O'Hara evokes deep and serious feelings about such a "decadent" subject. If O'Hara assumes Dean's voice at the end of "Four Little Elegies" it is to give Dean a lyric voice of his own, to grant him dignity without exaggerating his stature.

Dean's voice, rendered in short lines (either staggered or along one margin) suggests the shallow breathing of one barely alive. We overhear Dean pitying himself, but in a manner that is not merely self-pitying but also lyrical and soothing. What is most remarkable, however, is the way O'Hara achieves a kind of stammering lyricism here, appropriate to Dean's inarticulate adolescent presence on the screen. Mixing the lyrical with the slightly ludicrous he produces a voice for one to whom speech is still "too awesome a gift";

I breathe in the dust

        in my lonely room.

It may be a tree

        then why is there no bird?

There is no hand, pruning.

        Can you think of the sneeze

as a lovely thing? an apostrophe?

        Love is not gentle,

like the dust of a room;

        love is a thing that happens

in a room, and becomes dust.

        I breathe it in. Is that poetry?

                (251)

Indeed, the "dust" that love becomes may be poetry, but the meaning of Dean's question here is probably: is this passage poetry? The mixture of diction at times borders on the silly: "Can you think of the sneeze/ as a lovely thing?" But there is no denying the grace and cleverness of the aphorism that follows. As if surprised by his own eloquence, the naive speaker wonders if he has actually created poetry. Did he really fulfill his ambition to be a writer at last?

"Four Little Elegies" contains many interesting gradations and contrasts of tone and voice. The first section is a kind of epitaph for Dean, "WRITTEN IN THE SAND AT WATER ISLAND AND REMEMBERED," a title which echoes both John Keats's epitaph ("Here lies one whose name was writ in water") and Edmund Spenser's love lyric ("One day I wrote her name upon the strand"). Dean is an American product, naively ambitious, and, or course, "*stopped short.*" But the epitaph suggests that stopping short is best after all. This romantic idea, stated in a terse, dry way, adds up to a metaphysical joke: "*Do we know what/ excellence is?*" We cannot, because the function of excellence in "*this world*" is to remain in potentiality and never to be "*executed.*"

The tone of the second section, "LITTLE ELEGY," is both tender and humorous, modestly self-deprecating and yet ultimately sincere: "Let's cry a little while/ as if we're at a movie." For the first time in any of his elegies for Dean, O'Hara seems on the verge of acknowledging that his feeling partakes somewhat of the tearful affection we have for our favorite movie stars. Yet O'Hara also manages to convey the beauty of Dean's adolescent awkwardness, an image of "excellence" that is lovely for the very reason that it is still unformed: "He mumbled and scratched as if speech were too/ awesome a gift and beauty/ a thing you keep moving."

In section 3, "OBIT DEAN, SEPTEMBER 30, 1955," O'Hara adopts the voice of a newspaper obituary written by a sincere but ingenuous movie enthusiast who feels the need to repeat the sometimes trivial facts of Dean's life. He even asks Carole Lombard (the "patron saint" of all film stars who die young) to intercede on Dean's behalf in heaven. The obituary concludes by asserting that though Dean was in the public domain our affection for him is still private and close, as if he were a member of our family: "He's/ survived by all of us."

Part of the pathos of the obituary is that it makes Dean sound

like a failure, or at least like an unfulfilled man, despite his
meteoric success. But in the next section of the poem "A CERE-
MONY FOR ONE OF MY DEAD," O'Hara humorously undercuts the naive sweetness of the previous section, comparing his
grief to that of "so many gypsy girls who fell dead/ for love at
their tar-haired lovers' polished feet." Yet this comical, operatic
image of grief-in-unison prefigures what is to be the final movement of the poem, O'Hara's identification with Dean. Those of
us who survive Dean and mourn for him are seen in melodramatic
and even comic terms as overdoing it. The horrible rumor that
Dean is alive though "hideously maimed and hidden by a con-
scientious studio" (O'Hara is making fun of our queasiness
about injury and maiming) leads into the final sections where
O'Hara assumes Dean's voice from the grave, or the brink of the
grave.

Dean is a symbol of the ever-changing self, the vision of
the self that pervades O'Hara's poems. Adolescent and actor,
he was subject both to the changes in himself (his interest in turn
in movies, theater, literature, law, playing drums, riding motor-
cycles, racing cars) and to the actor's incessant changing of
roles. His name on the movie marquee finally becomes "the
big red/ calling-card of [his] own death." Death is, in a way,
yet another role for him. What makes O'Hara's identification
with Dean plausible is that O'Hara himself is playing roles in
the poem—speaking in various voices.

O'Hara's structure in "Four Little Elegies" is logical and
effective. The poem moves from a public view of Dean's death
to an intensely private identification with him, and the form
of address becomes more intimate in each section: from "we"
(Dean's public) to "I" (the poet as one of Dean's fans) to "you"
(addressed to Dean) and finally to the "I" which no longer
refers to the poet but to the poet and his subject together, both
O'Hara and Dean as they merge into one consciousness. Despite
this sequence the poem nevertheless conveys the impression of
a brilliant set of variations on a single theme. For it is only in
the interplay of these variations with their intricate and often
contrasting tones that the truth about Dean can be voiced.

Paradoxically, "Four Little Elegies" is O'Hara's best elegy for
Dean because of its unfinished, multivoiced, self-interrupting
quality. In essence, as the traditional elegiac poets have done,

O'Hara wants, ultimately, to deny the fact of death. But without recourse to the concept of heaven or an afterlife (or even, as Yeats had, a concept of man's place in history), O'Hara has to oppose death with mutability itself. Death for O'Hara cannot exist in a world in which we live, move and change. (Pollock, for example, in "Ode on Causality," is a living presence to O'Hara even when he is confronted with the stone and bronze fact of the artist's gravesite: he sees the "bronze JACKSON POL-LOCK/ gazelling on the rock.")

Oscillating between humor and pathos, O'Hara in "Four Little Elegies" is as serious as it is possible to be about immortality without really believing in it. Immortality, in his view, has nothing to do with man, though without man to imagine it there would be no immortality. "The heavens," as O'Hara said in "To the Film Industry In Crisis," "operate on the star system."

"The Day Lady Died" (O'Hara's elegy for "Lady Day," the singer Billie Holiday) is also an elegy rebelling against the elegiac tradition, a poem (like "The 'Unfinished'") full of irritating inconsequentialities. The poem is at last made beautiful and poignant, however, by its ending; O'Hara's strategy of avoiding the point throughout the poem becomes, finally, a way of getting at the truth.

Because of the title, we expect the poem to tell us about "Lady's" death. It begins, however, with what sounds like the voiceover sound track to a suspense movie: "It is 12:20 in New York a Friday." We expect, then, that this narrator will keep informing us of the minute events of the day as the clock ticks away towards the zero hour when disaster will strike. But we quickly realize that he has no interest in making these moments live. His narrative is totally devoid of sensation—not a word about how things feel, how he feels—except that at one point he "practically goes to sleep with quandariness" experiencing the sleepy numbness that comes over some people when they are nervous or tense. The narrator tells us nothing about how he feels as he walks around the city, yet he is so laboriously de-tailed about other matters. Who cares that Hesiod is "trans." by Richmond Lattimore? Though narrating the poem in the present tense, O'Hara cannot initially put us *in the moment* with him at all.

Holiday's death, as announced by the front page of the news-

paper, is the ingredient he needs to bring intensity and meaning
to all this triviality. Originally O'Hara referred to the heat with
the image of the "muggy street beginning to sun," but now we
can feel it with him: "I am sweating a lot by now." Along with
Holiday's picture, the heat is the medium that moves O'Hara
back in time to a moment that is much more real to him than the
flow of his present life. Up to now he has been moving busily
through the city, but his movements have had no meaning. Now,
however, he remembers a moment when he could hardly move
at all, "leaning on the john door in the 5 SPOT," immobilized
(along with everyone else) by the poignance of the ailing[4]
Holiday's "whispered" song.

O'Hara's narrative moves us through a diffused, distracted experience, where we are overwhelmed with unrelated details, to
a moment of breathless concentration on a single voice, a single
work of art. Tension of a certain kind can put him to sleep, but
awe, rapture, or any kind of deep attentiveness can suspend his
breathing and take him right out of time. The attention that art
claims for itself, O'Hara is telling us, makes time go away.

Only a poet with O'Hara's mastery of a talky-poetic style could
have fashioned a narrative such as this into a successful lyric.
O'Hara shifts his diction to make it a few degrees richer in
sound in the last stanza, though by no means changing completely from the prosey factuality of the earlier lines:

> and I am sweating a lot by now and thinking of
> leaning on the john door in the 5 SPOT
> while she whispered a song along the keyboard
> to Mal Waldron and everyone and I stopped breathing   (325)

In addition to the assonance, alliteration and rhyme in the
sequence "lot . . . leaning . . . spot . . . song . . . along," there   is
even a muted final cadence in the assonance of "keyboard" and
"breathing." Yet the transition is accomplished subtly, just as
O'Hara slides smoothly and naturally from his temporal narrative
to a moment outside of time.

The logic of the poem's construction seems clearer once we
can see how its seemingly trivial details both delay the elegiac
conclusion and also prepare for it. Such foreshadowings (like
all portents) are annoyingly indefinite, but they do prefigure the

ending: O'Hara's anxiety over dinner; the fact that it's "three days after Bastille Day" (a violent, revolutionary disappearance has occurred, but O'Hara is not aware of it yet); references to Ghana, and *Lés Nègres* by Genet (Holiday was black); the name of the bank teller, Linda Stillwagon (suggesting a hearse), and the fact that she forgets to check O'Hara's balance for the first time, a prefiguration of his loss of emotional equilibrium on learning of Holiday's death.

Yet details such as these seem too plainly factual to be intended as outright symbols. Indeed, the power of the ending is greater because it emerges from such impoverished, half-accidental materials. O'Hara's poem is both elegy and anti-elegy at once. In "The Day Lady Died" O'Hara writes an elegy that seems to interrupt itself but also fulfill itself in a moment of heightened emotion and transcendence—"I stopped breathing."

II *Friendship*

So much less intense and concentrated than feelings of passionate, obsessive love—so much less august, less defined, than feelings about death—feelings of ordinary friendship are among the most difficult to explore in a poem. Yet one of O'Hara's best poems, "Poem Read At Joan Mitchell's," is about friendship. As in his elegies, O'Hara's means of keeping the poem honest is through humor and through the diversionary tactics of digression. The poet is scrutinizing his own expressions of feeling, aware of the complex mixture of truth and excessiveness that makes up all declarations of affection, and this awareness makes his tribute seem all the more genuine, restrained, highly civilized, and loving.

O'Hara writes poems to friends as gifts, often as a way of commemorating specific occasions such as birthdays and engagements that are about to happen. He is interested in the way the fabric of his life consists of the many interlocking strands of his relationships, and he is conscious of finding himself at certain times at an important juncture in the history of a friendship. He celebrates these occasions, grasping at the elusive, shifting motion of the present moment, while at the same time tracing its connection with past and future. Whereas Yeats is magnificent in his ability to transform recollections of his friends into some-

thing approaching mythology,[5] O'Hara writes within the midst
of the ongoing history of a friendship. He renders the emotional
texture of the moment and that moment's participation in the
total relationship.

In "Poem Read At Joan Mitchell's" O'Hara alternates expressions of affection for his friends, and memoirs of good times
had together with remarks about his feelings at the instant he
is composing the poem or reading the poem aloud. Our attention
is drawn to the act of writing the poem (or reading it aloud)
and the gesture of friendship it implies, and we see him in the
very act of giving: "This poem goes on too long because our
friendship has been long .../ and I would make it as long as I
hope our friendship lasts if I could make poems that long..."
(266).

With this ingenious strategy we witness O'Hara *being a friend,*
saying the right loving words, patching up possible hurts and
misunderstandings, managing his aggressions, preparing an
acceptable self for the people he is fond of, and subordinating
his affection for other friends (not present) to his affection
for the friends who are present. It is like reading a letter; we
have to gauge how much the language is bending itself to
accommodate and charm the person to whom it is addressed. And
O'Hara, in weaving together the expression of feeling with the
occasion and context in which it is uttered, manages to give the
feelings just as much credibility as they deserve, and no more.
Feelings are not inflated into sentimental lies; they are seen by
the poet as being true-for-the-occasion. But they bespeak a core
of authentic affection which would be impossible to render
directly.

For example, in "John Button Birthday" O'Hara addresses
another friend:

> And then the way you straighten
> people out. How ambitious you are! And that you're
> a painter is a great satisfaction, too. You know how
> I feel about painters. I sometimes think poetry
> only describes. (267)

The love-flattery in these lines seems quite self-conscious. The
habit of straightening people out is not ordinarily likable (it

suggests self-righteousness), but O'Hara tactfully calls it "ambitious." Then too, as a deliberate tribute to Button, O'Hara degrades his own art in favor of his friend's. We move then to a passage that describes O'Hara alternately doing his laundry and writing more of the poem: "Now I have taken down the underwear/ I washed last night from the various light fixtures/ and can proceed." He accomplishes, albeit unconventionally, his needed chores, and we are reminded that friendship not only involves how we *feel* about others but also what we are willing to *do* for them. Feeling can be inferred from action.

"Poem Read at Joan Mitchell's" is the best example of such a strategy. Like Guillaume Apollinaire's "Poem Lu Au Marriage d'André Salmon" ("Poem read at the Marriage of André Salmon")[6] on which it is patterned, it was written to be read at a specific occasion—an engagement party for Jane Freilicher and Joe Hazan. O'Hara, "the decoy" for this surprise party attended by about ninety friends, contributed a poem, somewhat the same way a best man is often asked to make a toast. The poem serves as a script for O'Hara in wishing the couple well, but he also weaves into it a kind of scrapbook of reminiscences celebrating his friendship with Jane and Joe, and an account of his own ambivalent feelings about their forthcoming marriage.

Playing his role of toastmaster and constantly threatening to undermine it, O'Hara, from the outset, is wittily ambivalent about the joyous occasion, expressing his double opinion that marriage is both exciting and oddly oldfashioned, an adventure, but also a capitulation to the inevitable: "At last you are tired of being single/ the effort to be new does not upset you nor the effort to be other/ you are not tired of life together." The issue of boredom versus excitement, or convention versus innovation, is related to O'Hara's own mood:

Yesterday I felt very tired from being at the FIVE SPOT
and today I felt very tired from going to bed early and reading
    ULYSSES
but tonight I feel energetic because I'm sort of the bugle,
like waking people up, of your peculiar desire to get married   (265)

It is "dreary February" but O'Hara's tiredness could just as well be due to his own anxiety and depression about his friend Jane's marriage. (*Ulysses*, after all, is partly about the torments of adultery.) But then O'Hara claims to feel an infusion of new energy, like a bugle blowing reveille. Reciting his poem on "the day before February 17th," (Apollinaire, at least, was writing his poem on the day before Bastille Day, and could pretend that all the flags in the street were in honor of his friend), O'Hara sees Jane and Joe's marriage as a sign of spring. But the overriding question is whether this sign will be a sign for him too. Apollinaire, a heterosexual, could declare at the end of his poem: "Love which like light fills/ All solid space between the stars and the planets/ Love desires that my friend André Salmon should get married today." But for O'Hara the main issue is not married love, but happiness, his own as much as Jane and Joe's: "We peer into the future and see you happy and hope it is a sign that we/ will be happy too." He is worried, clearly, about the effect this marriage may have on his close, longstanding friendship with Jane Freilicher.

Like Apollinaire, O'Hara catalogues his memories of the friendship in the past. But Apollinaire's joy is due to his conviction that Love ("the director of fire and of poets") is manifesting itself through his friend's marriage; O'Hara, however, seems hopeful, but not entirely confident, that the friendship will continue as it was: "I hope there will be more." In listing the things he hopes there will be more of ("more evenings avoiding the latest Japanese movie ... more arguments over Faulkner's inferiority to Tolstoy") O'Hara not only reviews, scrapbook style, his friendship with Jane and Joe, their shared preferences and tastes, but also communicates his sense of being an outsider, a fifth wheel. He tells them "I should probably propose myself as a godfather if you have any children, since I will probably earn more money some day accidentally, and could teach him or her how to swim." But he has already said that Joe can beat him in a half-mile swim, and it is equally unlikely that this well-to-do couple will be forced to rely on him for money, even if he should "earn more ... accidentally." Significantly, he avoids any reference to his true value as a poet.

He calls to mind his two close friends, the poets John Ashbery and Kenneth Koch, and reminds his audience that Kenneth and John would have written differently had they been able to be present at the party. All of John's verses have a "nuptial quality,"

O'Hara explains, as he is always "marrying the whole world."
Kenneth, on the other hand, would write about the relationship
between men, women, and art. But while both of his friends
would have written in more general terms about the whole world
or about men and women, O'Hara's more modest approach is
to write about the particular occasion, and his own personal
situation: for him "ideas are obscure and nothing should be
obscure tonight."

O'Hara's anxiety resolves itself with the thought that while he
may be losing his friend Jane in some ways now that she and
Joe are getting married, he is not losing her completely: "you
will live half the year in a house by the sea and half the year
in a house in our arms." This image of compromise—recalling
the one arranged between Pluto and Ceres over Persephone (in
a myth accounting for the seasons)—has to be accepted, as one
must always accept the inevitabilities that time brings:

we peer into the future and see you happy and hope it is a sign that we
            will be happy too, something to cling to, happiness
the least and best of human attainments

Poignantly and beautifully O'Hara balances his anxieties and
doubts with hope. Happiness may also come to him. It may be
insignificant, depending as it does on so many unimportant
moments (drives to Bear Mountain and searches for hamburgers),
but it is also "best," and the poetry of happiness can be written
only by paying loving homage to such moments—both to the
moments of friendship in the past, and also to the moment that is
the occasion of the poem itself. Separated from his friends by
their impending marriage, he is nevertheless close to them because of the accumulated details of a shared past and present:

Tonight you probably walked over here from Bethune Street
down Greenwich Avenue with its sneaky little bars and the
    Women's Detention House

Unable to detain Jane Freilicher and keep her from becoming
Jane Hazan, O'Hara can at least cling to the wealth of particulars that is available to him at the moment. In signalling his
anxiety about what he stands to lose he can at least refer to

all that he has had. "Let's advance and change everything," he says, "but leave these little oases in case the heart gets thirsty en route."

Few poets could refer so ingenuously to the heart, giving voice to such "heart-felt" sentimentality. But O'Hara places these good wishes in the perspective of an actual, specific occasion. In allowing us to sense what he is evading he gives us an account of authentic feeling as well. The marriage of his friends may stem from something outside of O'Hara's sympathy, some "peculiar desire," but it is to be welcomed as all change is to be welcomed. O'Hara presents his loving gift, communicates his anxieties, and surmounts them, all in the course of his gracious, yet emotionally complicated, tribute to his friends.

III Love

Both the techniques used to express feelings in the love poems and the feelings themselves are meant to be simple and straightforward. O'Hara does not interrupt himself self-consciously or artfully digress as he does in his elegies, nor does he undercut his expression of affection for his lover, Vincent Warren, by calling attention to the act of writing poems for him, as he does in poems for friends. In the poems of death and friendship O'Hara undercuts his own expressions of feeling to avoid falseness, but in the love poems he knows that time itself will perform the task.

While O'Hara only included some of his poems for Vincent in his 1965 collection *Love Poems (Tentative Title)*, we can now read all of them in the order in which they were written.[7] From the prelude of the sequence, "Joe's Jacket" (August 10, 1959), which describes the first weekend O'Hara spent with Vincent, to "A Chardin in Need of Cleaning" (July 6, 1961), a poem in which O'Hara seems to be declaring the end of the relationship, it is possible to trace the entire arc of a love affair, from the initial exhilaration and bliss, to the period of deepest involvement, through a declining period of false or forced exuberance, to final feelings of hurt and bitter resignation to the inevitable. As with Shakespeare's *Sonnets* (though the problem here is not nearly so difficult, since almost all the poems are dated) a certain amount of speculation about the history of the relationship is necessary. But it is not important to know all the facts.[8] The poems illustrate O'Hara's love at various stages, and even more important, (whether or not O'Hara intended it) they comprise a true sequence.

Throughout the love poems we can sense an awareness on O'Hara's part of the temporary, fragile nature of his happiness. This awareness is expresed through images of light and darkness. As we recall, in "Joe's Jacket" O'Hara uses changes in light to evoke his changing feelings. In his first love poem explicitly to Vincent—an acrostic on Vincent's name—O'Hara describes an almost celestial moment of grace, free for a charmed moment from the passage of time: "the heavens' stars all out we are all for the captured time of our being" (331). The effect of love on him is registered in images which, though they cannot be permanent, seem to glow nevertheless like instants of "captured time."

Though the exhilaration of falling in love is ordinarily a shortlived emotion, O'Hara is able to sustain this exhilaration and evoke it in poem after poem by studying Vincent the way a painter studies a subject, not by trying to define what it is but by observing how the light transforms it. "Saint," an early poem for Vincent, opens with the following image:

> Like a pile of gold that his breath
> is forming into slender columns
> of various sizes, Vincent lies all
> in a heap as even the sun must rest   (332)

"Saint" comes closer than any other poem to giving us a portrait of Vincent as both a work of art and as a person. Vincent, a dancer, also thinks about his body as a work of art, though he is not yet quite satisfied with it. He is absorbed in trivial thoughts: "he is waiting for his sofa// to arrive from Toronto, that's what/ he thinks and of whether Maxine/ would like a pair of jet earrings." But Vincent's beauty, and his importance to O'Hara has nothing to do with what Vincent thinks, and O'Hara seems wittily aware of the disjunction between his worship of Vincent and his lover's mental shallowness. "So the night comes down," says O'Hara in conclusion, "upon/ the familial anxieties of Vincent/ he sleeps like a temple to no god." It does not matter that Vincent

is concerned about sofas, his body, earrings for Maxine—the very
fact of his physical existence is to be worshipped. In a later poem,
"Now That I Am In Madrid And Can Think," O'Hara expresses
this idea more strongly:

it's well known that God and I don't get along together
it's just a view of the brass works to me, I don't care about the Moors
seen through you the great works of death, you are greater

you are smiling, you are emptying the world so we can be alone
(356)

In Spain, away from Vincent, O'Hara sees Vincent as assuming
the role of a substitute God, "emptying the world" of all other
possibilities of significance, and becoming the only significant
being. Of course, O'Hara is humorously aware of the hyperbolic
nature of this declaration. Vincent supplants the importance of
God, with whom O'Hara does not "get along" anyway, and also
nullifies the masterpieces of art—"the great works of death."
But O'Hara is well aware that love has colored his perception
of the world; thanks to Vincent he is interested in light rather
than darkness, in life rather than death.

   Ultimately, this is the meaning of O'Hara's repeated use of the
imagery of light and dark. His love for Vincent is not merely
the unending admiration of an artist for his subject but also a
joyful light that suffuses the world and makes O'Hara see both
himself and life in a more optimistic way:

        ...I am dark
        except when now and then it all comes clear
        and I can see myself
        as others luckily sometimes see me
        in a good light   (335)

Or, as he says in "Variations on Pasternak's 'Mein Liebchen, Was
Willst Du Noch Mehr?'": "just the sight of you, no wall, no moon,
no world, makes/ everything day to me."

   But this light only exists in contrast to the darkness surround-
ing it. "The dark sky" is the background against which he and
Vincent, in the poem "To You," write the message of their love,

"like a couple of painters in neon." Moreover, this light can only be reached through darkness: "of light we can never have enough/ but how would we find it/ unless the darkness urged us on and into it" (335). In the love poems darkness stands for unhappiness and death, but it also stands for sexuality and mystery, especially the mystery of homoerotic love. In order to achieve the light, O'Hara also has to love the darkness, the sexuality which in the traditional theology of his Catholic upbringing is seen as evil. In psychological terms, lust can be the cause of faithlessness and betrayal as well: "I am dark," says O'Hara, but the faithlessness that is inherent in his own vision of himself is cancelled out "luckily sometimes" by those who, like Vincent, see the faithful and loving part of him.

This concept of love springing from the darkness of lust, but leading to joy and light reaches its culmination in "Present." The poem begins with an image of a snowy winter night in New York, near "the stranded gulch/ below Grand Central" (probably the Park Avenue underpass). For O'Hara, on this occasion, the city landscape is infused with thoughts of separation and loss:

> the gentle purr of cab tires in snow
> and hidden stars
>
>   tears on the windshield
> torn inexorably away in whining motion
> and the dark thoughts which surround neon   (352–53)

The "hidden stars," lights refracted from drops of melted snow on the windshield of a cab, return in a passage that expresses the inexorable law of physical separateness in space, a law which, because of their love, Frank and Vincent have suspended: "not like celestial bodies'/ yearly passes, nothing pushes us away/ from each other." The law of "celestial bodies" following their own orbits, and being pushed away from each other by the necessity of their individual fates, is also the law that, in O'Hara's bleak mood, seems to him to govern human relationships, a law that Vincent has suspended as far as Frank is concerned. In Vincent's presence the "dark thoughts" of "the quarrels and vices of/ estranged companions [which] weighed so bitterly/ and accidentally" seem dispelled.

Vincent once again is associated in this poem with light. O'Hara sees him first in Union Square, "red green yellow search-lights cutting through/ falling flakes, head bent to the wind/ wet and frowning, melancholy, trying." But in this case Vincent is not just a radiant piece of sculpture, but a human being with his own worries and problems. O'Hara leaves the final word "trying" indefinitely suspended, both verb and adjective, delicately suggesting that despite his love for him, Vincent too, like any other human being, can at times be "trying." But for both of them, whatever darkness surrounds them, it will lead to their meeting "in even greater darkness/ later." The "greater dark-ness," which at first seems to mean greater unhappiness, turns out to be the "warm" darkness of sexual contact and love. O'Hara's mood of depression, as it has been reflected in the wintry city landscape, becomes springlike when he touches Vincent; and he compresses this transition into lines in which his changed feel-ings about the world are, in a painterly way, visible to him in Vincent's expression: "your surprised gray look become[s] greener/ as I wipe the city's moisture from/ your face." The moisture of the melting snow also reminds O'Hara of the first time he saw Vincent "on/ the floor of my life walking slowly/ that time in summer rain stranger and/ nearer." Vincent at this point is both a "stranger" and immediately basic to O'Hara's happiness. The strangeness of Vincent is also part of the "peculiar" suspension of the dark laws of human separation; the "nearer" he comes, the "stranger" and more wonderfully unlikely it all is.

Helen Vendler has described "Having A Coke With You" as "one of the most beautiful of many [of O'Hara's] love poems."[9] Yet reading it in the context of the whole sequence of love poems, it is hard to overlook the fact that it was written immediately preceding a period in which O'Hara began to write poems doubt-ing his relationship with Vincent. "Having A Coke With You" does evoke, perhaps better than any poem in the language, what might be called a date mood. On a date (a really good one, that is) we try to focus on the person we are with as though to extract the maximum amount of pleasure from even the smallest details and gestures. As O'Hara concentrates on Vincent, all the paintings or sculptures they see (or do not see) become unimportant, no more than a backdrop.

This, of course, is a great compliment to Vincent (especially since O'Hara is a curator), and it is unlikely that O'Hara means to undercut its sincerity by making it all sound like mere affectionate flattery (as he might in a poem for a friend). O'Hara does qualify his enthusiasm momentarily by saying that he would rather look at Vincent than at all the portraits in the world *except* the *Polish Rider*, but luckily that is in the Frick and cannot spoil O'Hara's pleasure in Vincent by competing with him. In fact, the *Polish Rider* reminds O'Hara of yet another delightful museum he and Vincent should visit.

Unlike "Present," which melts together dreary weather and dreary thoughts with the warm, dark comfort of a tryst, "Having A Coke With You" is about "fun," about a "marvelous experience" which *is* fun and *is* marvellous for the very reason that it lacks full awareness of the possibility of pain and sadness in love, or even of mixed feelings.

As in past love poems, Vincent's beauty is associated with light—"in the warm New York 4 o'clock light we are drifting back and forth/ between each other like a tree breathing through its spectacles" (360). Explaining Vincent's beauty, or even describing it, would be as tedious and unnecessary as explaining why a sunny spring day is lovely. But such blithe joy is, however, too carefree to last. This is not mentioned, yet perhaps O'Hara is signalling such an awareness by deliberately confining his admiration for Vincent to aesthetics. The question of whether Vincent is or is not the "right person" seems to be as irrelevant to O'Hara as the identity of the person standing "near the tree" is to an impressionist painter whose only concern, after all, is points of light.

While "Having A Coke With You" is about simple joy, "Steps," the last of the exuberant love poems, is about infatuation: "all I want," O'Hara tells Vincent, "is a room up there/ and you in it." The poem's wit suggests excess and obsession. People stay together because their "surgical appliances lock"; the little box on the sidewalk is there "so the old man can sit on it and drink beer/ and get knocked off it by his wife later in the day/ while the sun is still shining." Even the heavy traffic exists for "people to rub up against each other," as O'Hara's imagination places love at the center of things, and imposes a uniform mood on the whole world: "the Pittsburgh Pirates shout because they won/

and in a sense we're all winning/ we're alive." The poem portrays
a mood of triumph and victory (O'Hara's days with Vincent are
called "V-days"), and O'Hara succeeds in buoyantly recasting
the city according to his own feelings. He seems to exult in the
fact that the "gay couple/ who moved to the country for fun/
. . . moved a day too soon" and his happiness seems to turn into
outright ferocity when he jokes that "even the stabbings are
helping the population explosion/ though in the wrong country."
Indeed, O'Hara's mood seems to be achieved only at the cost of
not caring about anyone or anything else, including himself:

> oh god it's wonderful
> to get out of bed
> and drink too much coffee
> and smoke too many cigarettes
> and love you so much   (371)

O'Hara sees his love for Vincent as being something like a delightful but compelling vice, and the poem communicates a
frenetic, nervous exuberance, rather than the tender fragile happiness of some of the earlier poems. In all, "Steps" is a kind of
gleeful celebration like the joy of the victorious baseball team
in front of the TV cameras.

Inevitably, such a stance introduces a certain shallowness into
the later love poems for Vincent that was not present at the
beginning. Poems such as "Vincent (2)" and "St. Paul and All
That" portray the love affair in its last stages, and show O'Hara's
circumspect awareness of the symptoms of waning interest and
declining happiness. In "Vincent (2)" a mere sigh from Vincent
disturbs him and makes him gloomy:

> this morning a blimp was blocking 53rd Street
> as inexplicable and final as a sigh
> when you are about to say why you did sigh
> but it is already done and we will never
> be happy together again never . . .   (402)

But Vincent turns up "in a gust of wind" and O'Hara's unhappiness, like the blimp that was blocking 53rd Street, "drifts
off into the blue theatre." "Why," he wonders, "did you sigh and

why did I notice." In the delight of their lovemaking "time collapses" and O'Hara laughingly confers on their tryst the title for a theatrical extravaganza: "the Palisades-Columbus-Avenue-Love-Bed-Awards."

In "Poem (Twin spheres full of fur and noise)," a poem describing lovemaking, O'Hara feels that his "mouth is full of suns." The light that O'Hara had earlier felt infusing the world is now concentrated on the exact moment of sexual bliss. Brilliantly and audaciously O'Hara renders the only light that remains for him:

> your hair is like a tree in an ice storm
> jetting I commit the immortal spark jetting
> you give that form to my life the Ancients loved
> those suns are smiling as they move across the sky
> and as your chariot I soon become a myth
> which heaven is it that we inhabit for so long a time
> it must be discovered soon and disappear   (405–6)

O'Hara marks this disappearance with a bitter joke. "I always said I was a shit," he seems to be telling Vincent in "A Chardin in Need of Cleaning"—"forearmed/ is foredefeated/ that's what Sherman really said." While O'Hara's love is firmly grounded in cynicism and self-doubt, Vincent's may not have been: "you didn't know," says O'Hara, "that the dark was sitting in your lap" (418).

But despite the inevitable closing in of darkness, O'Hara's love poems are not without their own kind of luminous victory. They evoke—as well as any poems in the language—moments of happiness in love when the mere presence of the beloved is enough to light up an otherwise dark world. Read in order, small differences of mood begin to take shape as part of a complex narrative of feeling. This "inside-narrative" of a love affair—from the initial infatuation to the final disillusionment—illustrates Kenneth Koch's assertion that O'Hara's *Collected Poems* can be seen as "a collection of created moments that illuminate a whole life" (*HF*, 208).

CHAPTER 6

Humor

What his work has always had to say to me, I guess, is to be more keenly interested while I'm still alive. And perhaps this is the most important thing art can say. ("Larry Rivers: A Memoir," 515)

ONE of O'Hara's foremost qualities as a writer is his sense of humor. When *Meditations in an Emergency* appeared in 1957, *The Saturday Review* particularly praised the humor of the poetry: "The humor is tender, the charm not in the least sticky, and the happiness never thoughtless."[1] The purpose of this chapter is to further describe and define O'Hara's use of humor, but also, ultimately, to identify the vision out of which it arises. O'Hara's poetry, as we have seen, asserts no systems of value and in his work neither the world nor the self have any intrinsic goodness or worth. Since this is so, the only justification for survival becomes our absurd, unjustifiable, but very palpable *wish* to. However self-amused and skeptical it may be, O'Hara's affirmation of life is an unquestioned first principle in his work, an essentially humorous but unwavering conviction, the equivalent of a moral attitude, and it is this that lies at the heart of his comic vision.

If affirmation is not always apparent in O'Hara's work it is because in well-known poems such as "Mary Desti's Ass" and "Ave Maria" O'Hara deflates what might usually be considered important issues into mere entertainment. This vision of life as entertainment approaches the Camp sensibility, as Susan Sontag defines it in "Notes on Camp": "The whole point of Camp," Sontag tells us, "is to dethrone the serious. Camp is playful, anti-serious. More precisely, Camp involves a new more complex relation to the 'serious.' One can be ... frivolous about the serious."[2] But while Sontag's notion of Camp precludes any

134

exploration of deep emotion, in works such as "Poem (The eager note on my door said, "Call me,")" beneath O'Hara's Camp detachment an undercurrent of emotional involvement can be felt. Camp (at least as Sontag describes it) is not a large enough term to encompass O'Hara's combination of playfulness and tragic awareness.

Self-deflation is also an important source of humor in O'Hara's poems. They register his amusement with the spectacle of his own impulsiveness and changeability. Often they are based on a tension between two alternate views of the self—humorously exaggerated self-aggrandizement undermined by modest self-deflation. In poems like "Louise" or "Autobiographia Literaria" we can see this tension at work, but it is only in more developed poems like "A True Account of Talking to the Sun at Fire Island" that O'Hara suggest the purpose of his self-deflation: survival. O'Hara renounces the dangerous temptation to be a godlike poet in favor of a view of himself as an ordinary, flawed creature who prefers the safer pleasures of ordinary life.

In poems where O'Hara's comic vision is most fully realized such as "Personal Poem," "To the Film Industry in Crisis," and "Poem (Khrushchev is coming on the right day!)," we can see the full movement: from Camp dismissiveness and comic deflation (as well as self-deflation) to a vision of affirmation—a commitment to life for its own sake.

I Deflation

Nonbeliever, homosexual, aesthete, O'Hara uses humor in his poetry to subvert conventional values, and to deflate the importance of anything that threatens to overshadow his own self-delighting movement through the world. As O'Hara says in "Meditations in an Emergency": "It is most important to affirm the least sincere" (197). This perhaps is another way of saying that it is most important to subvert the *most* sincere, the conventional values that O'Hara sees as interfering with life, and to affirm instead the Camp principle of having no principles at all.

This comic deflation applies to almost all areas of culture. Almost anywhere one looks in his poetry, O'Hara is bringing the high, the exotic, the famous, the aristocratic, even the sacred down to the homely level of everyday life:

I loll in bed reading *Poets of Russia*
("Poem [Dee Dum, dee dum, dum, dum, dee da]," 449)

one day the Via del Corso is named after [Gregory Corso]
("The 'Unfinished,'" 319)

...talking to a friend
who lunched with Dowager Queen Mary and offered
her his last cigarette...
("John Button Birthday," 267)

...the cartoon
            of a pietà
                        begins to resemble Ave Gardner
("Poem [I to you and you to me the endless oceans of]," 477)

Great as it is, Russian poetry can still be read in bed. O'Hara can imagine Rome's venerable Via del Corso retroactively named after his poet-friend Gregory. The Dowager Queen is not too aristocratic to be offered a cigarette. Even the Holy Mother bears an unsettling resemblance to Ava Gardner. Nothing escapes this leveling process—not even Nature, not even God himself:

rude snow fell and Lavoris-colored rain
("Captains Courageous," 452)

I am walking along the sidewalk
and I see a puddle and it's god, greedy god
always adding to yourself with raindrops and spit
we don't like that, god
("All That Gas," 324)

With an annoyed rebuke, O'Hara even brings "greedy god," who aspires to swallow up the entire universe, down to subhuman height.

This Camp dismissiveness, which declares everything equal, and nothing significant, can be one of O'Hara's most irritating qualities. His one-liner about T.S. Eliot—"I saw T.S. on the telly today. I find that he is one of the most intelligent writers of our 'day'" (467)—is mere nastiness, while the undifferentiated hodgepodge of 'personalities' in "Biotherm" is trivial and tiresome rather than humorous:

> as the clouds parted the New York City Ballet opened Casey
>   Stengel was there
> with Blanche Yurka, "Bones" Mifflin, Vera-Ellen and Alice
>   Pearce, Stuts
> "Bearcat" Lonklin and Louella "Prudential" Parsons in another
>   "box," Elsa
> "I-Don't-Believe-You're-a-Rothschild" Maxwell wouldn't speak
>   to them . . .   (445)

Yet some of O'Hara's best poems depend on the same Camp sensibility and deflation as the source of their humor.

In "Mary Desti's Ass," based on the autobiography of Mary Desti (a companion of the dancer Isadora Duncan), each stanza refers to a different incident in a different city around the world. Stanza by stanza, city by city, Mary Desti keeps up her endless, promiscuous travelling. For her, even the discovery of love amounts to no more than another "experience": "that was love," she tells us, "but I kept on traveling."

But to keep moving Mary Desti has to assume an aloof attitude towards whatever happens to her. Her favorite adjective is "amusing," and she applies it to experiences that most people would consider enervating and unpleasant. In Boston, she says, "I was usually lying/ it was amusing to be lying all/ the time for everyone." And in Singapore she gets a "dreadful/ disease," but says it was "amusing to have bumps/ except they went into my veins." What seems "amusing" to Mary Desti might well be considered traumatic. Yet the point about Mary Desti is the very evenness of her momentum. Her career is stifled ("I stepped in once/ for Isadora so perfectly/ she would never allow me to dance again"), but her only comment is "that's the way it was in Bayreuth."

Mary is still determined to explore her world, and her detachment at times fosters a sort of adventurous courage:

> now if you feel like you want to deal with
> Tokyo
> you've really got something to handle

> it's like Times Square at midnight
> you don't know where you're going
> but you know   (402)

Though it is important to know how to "handle" each city and each situation, some situations cannot be managed at all. In Tokyo, Mary simply has to trust to fate.

She has been squelched, hated, exploited, accosted by a furniture manufacturer, exposed to diseases, and bored by experiences that taught her nothing. But now the "glorious" experience of love touches her and seems, nearly, to penetrate her traveller's soul. Characteristically, her next observation is pure Camp: "that/ was love sneaking up on me .../ and I felt it was because of all/ the postcards and the smiles and kisses and the grunts." Love disintegrates into a collection of its external signs and gestures. Mary's "amusement" with love, however—her sudden deflation of what was "glorious"—is the very thing that allows her to keep on travelling. Like O'Hara himself, Mary sheds her feelings like old skins.

O'Hara's masterpiece of moral deflation is "Ave Maria," a mock sermon on the importance of letting children go to the movies. In this poem, O'Hara's humor does precisely what Susan Sontag claims Camp humor should. Camp deflates moral seriousness, and it acts, in Sontag's words, as a "solvent to morality. It neutralizes moral indignation, [and] sponsors playfulness" ("Notes on Camp," 290). Taking the opposite position from the Roman Catholic church, which at one time sought to shield even adults from the corrupting influence of the movies through its Legion of Decency, O'Hara exuberantly argues that parents owe it to their children to rescue them from innocence. Nor does O'Hara merely wish to confine the children's initiation to knowledge that comes from the screen; the children may also be seduced in the theater. The practical nature of such an initiation, which will "only cost [the parents] a quarter" and which will not "upset the peaceful home," has much to be said in its favor. And the children, O'Hara promises, will be so grateful.

O'Hara amusingly (and with some justice) takes for granted the hatred that is likely to spring up in "the little tykes" if they are sexually repressed, and his modest proposal is that parents simply (on behalf of better relations with their children) let

the children undergo their inevitable corruption without interfering with it. Like Swift advocating the practical advantages of
the poor marketing their extra children as veal, O'Hara advances
his argument as though it were, after all, nothing but common
sense:

> oh mothers you will have made the little tykes
> so happy because if nobody does pick them up in the movies
> they won't know the difference
> and if somebody does it'll be sheer gravy
> and they'll have been truly entertained either way
> instead of hanging around the yard
> or up in their room
> hating you
> prematurely since you won't have done anything horribly mean yet
> except keeping them from the darker joys   (372)

Playing with the usual idea of damnation, O'Hara asserts that
what is really "unforgivable" is keeping children from the
"darker joys" of sexual exploration. Making it all sound so whole-
some (if the children do get seduced it will be "sheer gravy")
O'Hara assures us, on the other hand, that keeping the children
away from the movies will lead to the breakup of the family. Like
children who masturbate (threatened with damnation in the
next world and blindness in this), repressed children kept from
the movies will go "blind in front of a TV set." O'Hara is simply
turning prudishness on its head here.

But unlike Swift's "A Modest Proposal," whose heart-chilling
advice is meant to invoke its own refutation, and which pre-
supposes a reader's essential humanity and compassion, O'Hara's
satire does not point to its own counter-argument at all. It
assumes in its good humored momentum, in its unpunctuated
barrage of witty logic, a world in which the good intentions of
parents to make their children good are doomed to failure, and
in which the only values to be affirmed are, as O'Hara says,
"the least sincere"—the values of entertainment and pleasure.
We all know, he seems to be winking at us, how hopeless it
is anyway. The sexuality the children are likely to be initiated
into, the illicit sexuality or homosexuality of the "pleasant
stranger whose apartment is in the Heaven on Earth Bldg,"

replaces the traditional heaven, and this reductive and unsettling ethic—the disagreeable side of the Camp sensibility—pervades the poem despite its seemingly carefree, celebratory tone.

But O'Hara's vision transcends the mere playfulness of Camp. While Camp, Sontag tells us, "refuses the risks of fully identifying with extreme states of feeling" (287), O'Hara's humor very often has a strong element of pain and tragic awareness.

O'Hara's brilliant "Poem (The eager note on my door said 'Call me,')" may seem at first to achieve nothing but an emotional stalemate. O'Hara presents his friend's suicide as a kind of overelaborate melodrama, and in this way seems to be defending himself against any possible guilt. "I did appreciate it," he says of his friend, his would-be host, who is lying in the hall on a "sheet of blood." His friend has certainly gone to extravagant lengths to roll out the red carpet, but an ironic appreciation of this is the only reaction O'Hara seems to be allowing himself.

Perhaps he is trying to avoid feeling responsible for the death? After all, he has mistaken the purpose of the "eager note" by assuming it to be a social, even sexual invitation rather than a plea for help. He does not call, as the note requests, but simply packs his "overnight bag" and starts out. But he arrives too late and finds his friend dead. His only defense against implicating himself is to pretend he is indeed impressed by such overzealous hospitality. Committing suicide all over the hallway! How stagy! "If tragedy is an experience of hyperinvolvement," Sontag tells us, then "[Camp] comedy is an experience of underinvolvement, of detachment" (288).

But is O'Hara really so uninvolved as he pretends? Clearly, the emotional impact of this disturbing poem originates in something O'Hara *is* suggesting about his feelings. But to read his message we have to pay careful attention to his movements. At the outset, on receiving his friend's invitation, he is both in a hurry—"I quickly threw/ a few tangerines into my overnight bag,/ straightened my eyelids and shoulders, and/ headed straight for the door"—and terribly slow: "It was autumn/ by the time I got around the corner... (14). While he has been hurrying to be with his friend time has been rushing by even faster, just as it does when we think we are in a hurry to get to a place we would really prefer not ever to arrive at. On an errand of life, to paraphrase Melville's "Bartleby," O'Hara seems to be aware that he is speeding towards death.

Though O'Hara insists on a deflated, life-as-melodrama version of his friend's suicide, the feeling of dread in this poem originates in the loss of his dreamy gaiety and come-what-may impulsiveness. His friend, whom he calls a "champion jai-alai player," is playing a dangerous game in appealing to someone this ambivalent, impulsive and unstable. But O'Hara's friend has arranged to trap him with a sobering tableau, bringing his spontaneous and carefree existence to a standstill. The blood "runs" down the stairs, but O'Hara is left standing there transfixed by his host.

Few moments in O'Hara's poems have the impact of this ending. His pose of indifference is subtly undermined and his true response can be felt by the way he structures his narrative, ending it at the moment he is forced to confront his friend's rage and despair. O'Hara has not quite survived the confrontation. The tone of ironic distance seems not so much dismissively Campy as bravely understated. O'Hara *is* affected. He is trying to deflate the tragedy with a joke, but it has been his tragedy as well, and the poem leaves us uncertain about whether he will ever be able to leave behind the traumatic scene he has witnessed and resume his carefree movement through the world.

"Poem (The eager note . . .)" is by no means humorous, though it uses humor to intensify the ultimate impact of events on the poet-narrator. Often, however, in O'Hara's overtly humorous poems, what passes for cheerfulness represents, in fact, a tough stance against adversity.

For example, even in an urban pastoral like "The Lay of the Romance of the Associations" (a poem dedicated to Kenneth Koch and very much like the kind of fantasy Koch handles with such sweetness) O'Hara's purpose is not to transport himself or us to a better or more beautiful world, as Koch's poems frequently do. Though the poem proposes a love affair between Fifth Avenue and Park Avenue (who are, however, separated by stern, bourgeois Madison Avenue) the result is as much a satire as an idyll. Fifth Avenue proposes to Park Avenue: "Why don't we rendezvous in Central Park behind a clump of cutthroats." And even the upbeat final thought—"there we'll kiss and hold each other/sweatily as in a five o'clock on a mid-August Friday in the dusk/ and after, languorously bathe, to sweeten city water for all time" (321)—brings to mind the heat of New York summers and the bad water. In O'Hara's work, in general, no city is without dirt, no love without pain. O'Hara may deflate the "seriousness" of certain problems, but he remains aware of them; his work is grounded in reality and his affirmation of life is not based on a mere denial of the unpleasant truth.

II *Self-deflation*

Whether he is engaged in true moral subversion as in "Ave Maria," or only putting on a brave act as in "Poem (The eager note . . .)," O'Hara's deflation of issues and problems is accompanied by self-deflation as well. Neither the world, nor the self that is always changing chameleonlike within it, is entitled to any pretentions of grandeur. As O'Hara says in "Joe's Jacket": "no central figure me, I was some sort of cloud or a gust of wind/ at the station a crowd of drunken fishermen on a picnic." Whitman, too, celebrated his ability to merge with a crowd, and to become part of what he was observing, but while Whitman cultivates a cheerful, expansive self-pride, O'Hara likes to direct his irony towards himself:

> . . . the slush is like my
> heart leading through
> little paths and puddles
> to a delicatessen or theatre
> ("Poem [It was snowing and now]," 383)

and do I really want a son
to carry on my idiocy past the Horned Gates
poor kid   a staggering load
("Cornkind," 387)

> Quick! a last poem before I go
> off my rocker . . .
> ("On Rachmaninoff's Birthday," 159)

you were made in the image of god
I was not
I was made in the image of a sissy truck driver
("Naptha," 338)

Though, as Stuart Byron points out, a "sissy truck driver" might be the ideal thing to be in O'Hara's homosexual milieu, O'Hara begins with the traditional (and more lofty) view of man as being made in God's image and then collapses it. Characteristically, O'Hara moves from self-inflation to comic self-deflation.

In "Louise," a poem about a louse O'Hara thought he saw on his own "immaculate person one day" (540) we follow the "tiny figure" as she makes her way up the poet's body. O'Hara observes himself from a louse's viewpoint—the vast rolling plain of his own stomach, the "crater of his navel, the "Twin Peaks" of his nipples "with the scattered/ forests coming right to the edge/ of the pass." Seen from Louise the Louse's perspective O'Hara's reaction to her presence is much like that of an angered God. After this "earthquake," Louise is stranded eye-to-eye with O'Hara—"a speck, and a vastness staring/ back at it."

The louse reminds O'Hara of Maldoror. In *Les Chantes de Maldoror*, one of God's giant hairs—terrifyingly huge—is abandoned in a whorehouse. Lautréamont's theme (that God is every bit as loathesome as man, probably more so) receives an interesting transmutation in O'Hara's poem. Here man is seen as both godlike and cheerfully louselike as well. In a moment of delightful comic deflation O'Hara, after allowing Louise to hover in his "blue/ gaze," decides in astonishment that he recognizes the louse from previous meetings and gives her a friendly hello: "Why it's Louise! Hi, Louise." Not only is O'Hara friendly to Louise, but he even acknowledges the louse's equality by calling into question his own authority to narrate: "the toiling figure," he says of Louise, "suddenly finds itself in a clearing. (Suddenly to me!)" There are *two* conceptions of time and space involved in this confrontation. (After all, Louise may have her own account of the affair.) As the intermediate link in the "chain of being" O'Hara seizes the comic opportunity of suddenly collapsing himself from a godlike creature to one who is on familiar terms with the very insects that infest him.

In O'Hara's "Autobiographia Literaria" the movement seems to be from humility to self-pride; but in fact, the poem reverts back to humility through O'Hara's skillful use of overstatement. As Marjorie Perloff suggests, O'Hara's poem humorously reverses Wordsworth's vision of the child as being closer to nature, and coming into the world "trailing clouds of glory."[3] From being off

in a corner, rejected by both male and female as well as animals,
O'Hara moves to what seems to be a position of exalted
centrality:

> When I was a child
> I played by myself in a
> corner of the schoolyard
> all alone.
>
> I hated dolls and I
> hated games, animals were
> not friendly and birds
> flew away.
>
> • • • •
>
> And here I am, the
> center of all beauty!
> writing these poems!
> Imagine!   (11)

But we can sense, from the overabundance of exclamation points,
that O'Hara is also mocking the poet's tendency to get carried
away by his own gifts. In this final affirmation of his adult powers
as a poet—so overexcited, so startled—we can see what is to
become O'Hara's characteristically self-deflating attitude. In
one sense, O'Hara is suggesting that the poet is less worthy and
important than his poetry. Though his poems place him at
"the /center of all beauty" it is hard for him to believe that the
poem originates in his own humble self. As the bare simplicity
of this little poem conveys with its charmingly understated pathos
("animals were/ not friendly"), the poet's consciousness is still
partly that of the child. The genius he finds himself graced with
seems to have descended upon him like some unfathomable
accident.

Ultimately, the purpose of O'Hara's self-deflation is survival.
This can best be seen by comparing O'Hara's wonderful "A True
Account of Talking to the Sun at Fire Island" to the Russian
poem on which it is based: "An Extraordinary Adventure Which
Befell Vladimir Mayakovsky in a Summer Cottage."[4] In Maya-
kovsky's poem the poet portrays himself on a heroic scale, and

both the poet and the sun are rather fierce and dangerous. The poet, driven into an immense rage by the daily rising and setting of the sun, invites the sun to tea, but when he sees the sun coming across the field he is stricken with fear:

> "You called me?
> Give me tea, poet,
> Spread out the jam!"
> Tears gathered in my eyes—
> The heat was maddening,
> But pointing to the samovar,
> I said to him:
> "Well, sit down then,
> Luminary!"

Difficult as it may be to gauge the difference in tone between an English and a Russian poem, it seems clear that in O'Hara's "A True Account of Talking to the Sun at Fire Island" the sun is a more informal, less frightening being. And the poet, more timid than Mayakovsky, had no thought of summoning him:

> The Sun woke me up this morning loud
> and clear, saying "Hey! I've been
> trying to wake you up for fifteen
> minutes. Don't be so rude, you are
> only the second poet I've ever chosen
> to speak to personally
>   so why
> aren't you more attentive? If I could
> burn you through the window I would
> to wake you up. I can't hang around
> here all day."

O'Hara's answer—"Sorry, Sun, I stayed/ up late last night talking to Hal"—also has a disarming modesty (though he does seem to assume the sun knows who "Hal" is, just as he likes to assume his readers know his friends by their first names). The sun's off-hand manner of speaking, and its use of puns—"Frankly I wanted to tell you/ I like your poetry"—convey a feeling of comical informality. While Mayakovsky raises himself to the sun's level, O'Hara brings the sun down to his own. The sun admits its in-

ability to burn O'Hara through the window. And the sun's
advice to O'Hara follows its own amusing, downward arc
with its disappointing qualifications:

> "always embrace things, people earth
> sky stars, as I do, freely and with
> the appropriate sense of space. That
> is your inclination, known in the heavens
> and you should follow it to hell, if
> necessary, which I doubt."   (306–7)

Rather patronizingly, the sun tells O'Hara to "Go back to sleep
now/ Frank, and I may leave a tiny poem/ in that brain of yours
as my farewell." But O'Hara's "tiny poem"—for all its self-
deprecating modesty—has a large theme.

Mayakovsky, at the end of his poem, assumes a very brave
stance:

> to shine
> and to hell with everything else!
> that is my motto—
> and the sun's!

But while Mayakovsky aspired to have the same radiant independence as the sun, he later committed suicide, unable to live
out his life in the face of personal and political frustrations.
O'Hara, however, is less dangerously self-aggrandizing: "You
may/ not be the greatest thing on earth, but/ you're different,"
the sun tells him. And it is O'Hara's difference from his predecessor Mayakovsky that is especially important here. The myste-
rious "calling" of the poet can, as in Mayakovsky's case, be associated with the summoning of death. Unlike Mayakovsky,
who resolved to go on shining like the sun, O'Hara is aware of
the dark significance of taking the sun as a symbol of oneself:

> "Sun, don't go!" I was awake
> at last. "No, go I must, they're calling
> me."
>   "Who are they?"
>   Rising he said "Some

> day you'll know. They're calling to you
> too." Darkly he rose, and then I slept.　　　　　(307)

O'Hara realizes that comparing the light of poetic talent within oneself to the light of the sun means also reckoning with the inevitable coming of darkness and one's own death. He too is proud of himself, but within the bounds of human rather than superhuman expectation.

O'Hara, unlike Mayakovsky, knows the danger of the heroic pose, and prefers instead the pose of the self-deprecating comic hero. While Mayakovsky is initially the sun's challenger (and then, at least, wants to shine along with him) O'Hara is content to receive the sun's avuncular advice and when comforted and relieved slips peacefully off to sleep. This sleep may be a prefiguration of death, but O'Hara is willing to leave that in the hands of fate. Unlike Mayakovsky he rejects any inclination to soar off into the heavens only to meet a tragic end.

III　*Affirmation*

Casting extraneous morality and seriousness aside, puncturing any dangerous tendency to self-inflation, O'Hara clears a space for what he considers of true importance—an affirmation of life itself. He can only be sure he loves his life (or at least that he loves it at the moment) if he first rejects all the proper and serious reasons for such love. In O'Hara's most fully realized comic poems, deflation (and often self-deflation) leads to affirmation.

"Personal Poem" illustrates this movement. With its "I do this I do that" structure and its unpunctuated, run-on (and . . . and . . . and) all-in-one-breath momentum, it glides over issues which O'Hara refrains from focusing on, lest they depress him:

> 　　　　　. . . I wait for
> LeRoi to hear who wants to be a mover and
> shaker the last five years my batting average
> is .016 that's that, and LeRoi comes in
> and tells me Miles Davis was clubbed 12
> times last night outside BIRDLAND by a cop
> a lady asks us for a nickel for a terrible

> disease but we don't give her one we
> don't like terrible diseases, then
> we go eat some fish and some ale . . .   (335–36)

The swift, unpunctuated flow of his experience goes on, not ignoring his or the world's problems, but not dwelling on them either, insisting on the comic principle of continuation rather than the tragic principle of disaster: "I shake hands with LeRoi/ and buy a strap for my wristwatch and go/ back to work happy . . ."

In asserting the importance of his own personal happiness over the more remote societal and political events that are important to LeRoi, or over that remote "terrible disease" that neither of them "likes" enough to contribute a nickel to, O'Hara is subverting ordinary morality, and its accompanying statistics, and replacing it with a more personal kind of reckoning. Worldly success ("my batting average/ is .016"), racial violence ("Miles Davis was clubbed 12/ times"), a nickel to cure a "terrible disease"—none of this weighs as much in O'Hara's moral reckoning as the "one person out of the 8,000,000" inhabitants of New York who might be thinking of him at that particular moment, and with whom O'Hara is in love.

Happiness depends upon having the wisdom to narrow things down—to rely only on essentials: "Now when I walk around," O'Hara begins, "I have only two charms in my pocket." More than any good luck charm, ancient or modern, valuable or worthless, more than magical silver hats and the glory of walking on girders, O'Hara values his everyday life and work in New York—provided that this life also offers the possibility of love. In "Personal Poem" O'Hara may dismiss what other people value, but he ultimately affirms a moral attitude of his own. "We/ don't like terrible diseases," he says with a Campy illogic, as though the disease were being offered to him for his appreciation (or for him to catch). But his rejection of the terrible keeps him free—as a good luck charm might—to enjoy life itself.

In O'Hara's best poem on the movies, "To the Film Industry in Crisis," he begins by denying the charm of the more "serious" forms of entertainment (literary quarterlies, experimental theater, grand opera, the Catholic Church, the American Legion) and then asserts his love for the movies. Yet in affirming the movies as the true cosmic entertainment, O'Hara also seems to be mocking them. The tone is not simply one of praise or of satire, but of both. Film does enshrine certain luminous gestures forever. It makes "stars" out of mere human beings, and the "star system" of film becomes O'Hara's half-humorous, half-serious symbol for the eternal. It is a symbol full of richness to him precisely because it participates both in the eternal realm of art and in the banal world of everyday life. It is the banality of the movie stars, sometimes even their lack of any special talent to be anything other than themselves, that is most appealing to him. Here is an art which has all the frailty of the present instant, and yet it will also last far into the future as the embodiment of a lost world. Though the over-all movement of the poem is towards genuine affirmation, O'Hara's enthusiasm is convincing precisely because he humorously acknowledges the fragile triviality of the movies as well.

O'Hara's use of the Homeric list for a mock heroic effect emphasizes this double perspective. The movies, O'Hara suggests, provide us with a whole array of eternal beings who, like the Greek gods, are not particularly virtuous or admirable, but who have unchanging essences. O'Hara, in one long list like those in Homer's *Iliad*, cites two dozen or so of such beings. O'Hara loves them and seeks to enshrine them all, regardless of talent or importance: "To ... the Tarzans, each and every one of you (I cannot bring myself to prefer/ Johnny Weissmuller to Lex Barker, I cannot!)" Though he is mimicking the breathless enthusiasm of a movie addict, O'Hara is not exactly mocking the film industry with his indiscriminate declaration of loyalty and love. He is suggesting that the movies provide an alternate world which is human in form but eternal and luminous, something like the realm of the gods on Mt. Olympus, or the eternal space inhabited by Homer's heroes. Enshrined here are ordinary, insignificant gestures, and the world of the movies is a world in which the ordinary has been made into the eternal: "Sue Carroll [*sic*] ... sits for eternity on the damaged fender of a car/ and smiles ..." The movies magnify and illuminate the "frail instant" (232) and preserve it.

What attracts him to the movies, and what he renders so delightfully in this poem of praise, is the combination of the inconsequential and the memorable. Nothing of what the stars

are or do is especially worthy in itself, except the perfection with
which they embody certain characteristics and certain gestures.
"Peach-melba-voiced Fred Astaire of the feet" is no better or
worse than Mae West with her "bordello radiance and bland
remarks"; they are each perfectly themselves on the screen. And
"Clark Gable rescuing Gene Tierney from Russia" is no more or
less important than "Allan Jones rescuing Kitty Carlisle from
Harpo Marx." This witty equation which substitutes Harpo Marx
for Russia illustrates the great advantage of the movie world:
since nothing is of any consequence, absolutely everything is.
No matter how similar the stars are, no two are quite interchangeable, whether it is "Gloria Swanson reclining," or "Jean
Harlow reclining and wiggling," or "Alice Faye reclining/ and
wiggling and singing." And in the world of the movies the
"stunning urbanity" of William Powell reflects no more or less
credit upon him than the "flaming hair and lips and long, long
neck" of Jeannette MacDonald. Physical and moral attributes
are equivalent in a world that is all luminous surface. The
movies create a world that is loveable and poignant despite the
fact that gestures of despair and elation are never more than
gestures, just frames in the endless reel: "Cornel Wilde coughing
blood on the piano keys while Merle Oberon berates,/ Marilyn
Monroe in her little spike heels reeling through Niagara Falls,/
. . . and Dolores del Rio/ eating orchids for lunch and breaking
mirrors."

Though it too, like "Ave Maria," seeks to replace heaven with
the movies, "To the Film Industry in Crisis" is more whole-
somely pagan in spirit than it is antiChristian. Written in 1955,
at a time of crisis for the major studios (due to the rise of
television and financial mismanagement) the poem is both ironic
and loving. It builds on a Camp tenderness for the excessive
and the artificial, but becomes a poem of love and praise; it
becomes, in its own way, a moral statement, affirming entertainment as the world's reason for being. The important thing,
O'Hara implies again and again, is to approve the way in which
life, like the movie world, goes on and on.

In "Poem (Khrushchev is coming on the right day!)," when
O'Hara weaves his own experience walking around New York
together with that of Khrushchev, the world leader, and celebrates
it as being all part of the ongoing motion of the world on a

delightful windy autumn day, he is committing himself to a vision of affirmation that is rare in contemporary literature:

New York seems blinding and my tie is blowing up the street
I wish it would blow off
                         though it is cold and somewhat warms
                               my neck
as the train bears Khrushchev on to Pennsylvania Station
     and the light seems to be eternal
     and joy seems to be inexorable
     I am foolish enough always to find it in wind   (340)

O'Hara finds joy in the slight thawing of the Cold War, even in his necktie (because it keeps his neck warm), and especially in the wind which is a sign of the motion and change that he most loves to observe and celebrate. But perhaps most of all he finds joy in the foolishness of his own mood which allows him to find a place even for Khrushchev in the ongoing procession of his own happy thoughts. The importance of the visit of the world leader is reduced to that of some kind of delightful happening (like a blimp flying over the city) but at the same time it is elevated in importance as a personal symbol for O'Hara (who had recently met and fallen in love with Vincent Warren) of the inebriating joy that comes from the collapse in barriers between one person and another when falling in love.

The essential elements of O'Hara's comic vision are all here: O'Hara deflates the importance of "important" subjects (though in this case he gives Khrushchev's visit a warmer, more personal significance); he deflates, also, the importance of himself ("I am foolish") in order to portray himself as a modest, comic hero determined to continue living and enjoying his life despite his awareness of evil and darkness hovering on the periphery. ("Where," he asks, "does the evil of the year go/ when September takes New York?")

It may be that O'Hara's affirmation of the world as a source of joy is no more fundamentally correct than Vincent's preference for Ionesco over Beckett, or, for that matter, no more significant than a preference for "blueberry blintzes." But the delight of the poem—expressed so well with O'Hara's typographical choreography (the whole poem is like a sidewalk

ballet)—is irrepressible and inevitable. Yet it is poignant too,
since it takes place against a backdrop of darkness and an awareness of evil: "the light *seems* to be eternal/ and joy *seems* to be
inexorable." It is not, of course. But O'Hara's foolishness in
believing it is—his response to the wind, to the rush of feeling
within himself—has a certain wisdom.

As he says in "Adieu to Norman, Bon Jour to Joan and
Jean-Paul":

> the only thing to do is simply continue
> is that simple
> yes, it is simple because it is the only thing to do
> can you do it
> yes, you can because it is the only thing to do

This is not a statement of simple optimism: the bleakness of
the oft repeated phrase "the only thing to do" tells us that.
In this internal conversation (where questions are not really
questions, and answers are not really answers) the only certain
thing is a kind of absurd faith that

> ... surely we shall not continue to be unhappy
> we shall be happy
> but we shall continue to be ourselves everything continues
>   to be possible
> René Char, Pierre Reverdy, Samuel Beckett it is possible isn't it
> I love Reverdy for saying yes, though I don't believe it   (329)

Neither Char nor Reverdy is a comic poet; it was Reverdy who
once affirmed (with implications that are darker than O'Hara's):
"Everything continues/ No one knows where time will stop/
Or night."[5] But O'Hara's poem seems, more pertinently, to be a
response to Samuel Beckett's comedy of continuation, *Waiting
for Godot*. Beckett's characters in this play, Vladimir and Estra-
gon, continually return to the despairing refrain "Nothing to be
done." But the end of the play sees them continuing on very
much as they were. They too seem to realize that to continue is,
after all, "the only thing to do." Like that of Beckett, like that
of the best modern comic writers, O'Hara's affirmation of the
capacity of human beings to survive despite their confusion,

boredom, and pain is not at all a matter of simplicity—it is a decision. O'Hara may not believe in affirmation, but he decides to love it. This comic gesture implies the kind of "foolish" hope that, to certain minds, may ultimately be the most plausible, the *only* plausible faith.

CHAPTER 7

Conclusion

*. . . Oh be droll, be jolly
and be temperate! Do not*

*frighten me more than you
have to! I must live forever.*
("The Critic")

IT is difficult to predict how great an influence Frank O'Hara's
poems will have in the future, or whether he will, as he
himself believed, "live forever." But for one answer, at least,
we can turn back to Pasternak, with whom we began. At the
conclusion of *Dr. Zhivago* certain notes are found among the
papers of the poet-hero of the novel, Yuri Zhivago: "I live,"
he writes, "at a busy intersection. Moscow, blinded by the sun
and the white heat of its asphalt-paved yards, scattering reflec-
tions of the sun from its upper windows, breathing in the flow-
ering of the clouds and streets, is whirling around me, turning
my head and telling me to turn the heads of others by writing
poetry in its praise."[1]

Though Pasternak's Zhivago may not have written the urban
poetry he recognized as "the living language of our time"
(*Zhivago*, 488), his writings are infused with the atmosphere
of the city in which he lived—Moscow. In the final moments of
the novel a book of Zhivago's poems is being read by two men
who knew him, and had known his poems for years. As they sit
and read at an open window overlooking Moscow, they are
"enveloped by the unheard music of happiness that flowed all
about them and into the distance. And the book they held
seemed to confirm and encourage their feelings" (*Zhivago*, 519).

A poet lives on in others because of the feelings he encourages
them to recognize. In Zhivago's case, as in O'Hara's, these

154

feelings have to do with the "unheard music of happiness" that flows through the city in which he lived, and we can detect this note in the works of younger New York poets:

SATURDAY ON THE WEST SIDE OF ASSISI

Saturday morning put on a record make coffee
and dance in front of the mirror
You're not Fred Astaire but you'll do
as you whisper "I love I love I lo-ove her!"
but whom do you love, remember?
Saturday. Only Saturday.
The coffee smells good and you know exactly when to turn it off.

Sip it on a stuffed chair looking at the thin light
spoon itself, like sugar, onto the dusty rose carpet
Those special pink dyes only the Chinese know—
This isn't one of them.
Can't get rugs like that out of Peking any more.

Later you water the plants and walk to the lake
Watch the long-distance runners with numbered orange tee shirts
and the slow lazy couples who have just got up from sex,
cruising the windows of antique shops for a lamp.
You come back home and read a long numbing article
in The New York Review of Books on Conrad
By that time it will be three o'clock and you've
run out of momentum. Time to make new decisions
get on the phone: Who wants to go to the movies tonight?

This is my life. I have no complaints.
If I were a family man I could spend weekends responding
to my children's cuts and yells,
never have to think too far in advance. Maybe lock myself
in the rec room for hours reading every word of Proust.
No, I'd be happy.
Granted that much to the future.
The birds
would hop above my deckchair in what suburban sunset?
But the birds sing even on West 71st Street,
and I am Saint Francis of Assisi.

—Phillip Lopate[2]

Here is a different voice, linguistically and emotionally more sober than O'Hara's. (Lopate begins with a joyful burst of run-on sentences, as O'Hara might. But it isn't long before stark, almost laconic rhythms take over: "This is my life. I have no complaints.") Lopate seems to be a man who is conscious of living within strict limits. He has at best something of a stoical optimism, and joy comes to him, like the light, in precious spoonfuls of sugar. He is also aware (much more so than O'Hara) of the limitations of the life he does *not* lead. Married life hovers in his mind as a very palpable alternate existence. (O'Hara never went very far in this direction; at most—in "Poem Read at Joan Mitchell's"—he imagines teaching other people's kids how to swim.) Yet clearly O'Hara's poetry has contributed to Lopate's sensibility in this poem and to his celebration of his singleness and of his urban life.

We can feel O'Hara's presence in this poem in the "I do this I do that" form it takes, and in the soft relevance, and/or irrelevance, of its details. (The rugs that cannot be gotten from Peking anymore, for example, could be a symbol of the limitations of any one life-choice, and yet the reference seems more informal than that—a little mental sidetrip.) But the borrowing of a form is less important here than the feelings that seem to have become recognizable and definite with O'Hara's help: the ordinary dancing-around morning happiness (much like O'Hara's in "Beer for Breakfast": "It's the month of May in my heart as the song/ says . . ."); the eager, slightly voyeuristic pleasure of touring Central Park (recalling O'Hara's notation in "Steps": "everyone's taking their coat off/ so they can show a rib-cage to the rib-watchers/ and the park's full of dancers . . ."); the willingness to name even the dreariest detail from amongst the glut of city information, even a "long numbing article" on Conrad in the *New York Review* (reminiscent of O'Hara's quandary over "Hesiod, trans. by Richmond Lattimore" in "The Day Lady Died"); the recognition of the all-importance (and the annoyance) of making dates with friends for the evening to prevent boredom (as in O'Hara's "Metaphysical Poem"); and finally, and most importantly, a secular joy so intense it resembles religious beatitude, the joy Lopate finds in his birds, and that O'Hara is "foolish enough/ always" (340) to find in the wind. Lopate's is the same skeptical celebration we find in O'Hara, the same almost-surprised affirmation of city pleasures, and, above all, the same exhilaration on finding that this happiness is being reflected back by the city landscape. The feelings Lopate is registering here (without sacrificing the individuality of his own sensibility) are among the feelings O'Hara's poems "confirm and encourage."

Just as securely as Zhivago's world is Moscow, O'Hara's is New York; and no American poet of city life will escape some debt to O'Hara in the future. But O'Hara has also given us exceptional poems about love ("Ballad," "Present"), about art ("Ode on Causality," "Why I Am Not A Painter"), about dance ("Ode to Tanaquil Leclerq"), about music ("Lisztiana"), about film ("To the Film Industry in Crisis," "Fantasy"), about friendship ("Larry," "Poem Read at Joan Mitchell's"), about growth and initiation ("Poem [There I could never be a boy]," "River"), about homosexual life ("Homosexuality," "Grand Central," "Song"), about death ("Four Little Elegies," "The Day Lady Died," "A Step Away from Them"), and about the ongoing process of life itself ("Ode to Michael Goldberg," "Joe's Jacket," "Adieu to Norman, Bon Jour to Joan and Jean-Paul")—to name but a few.

In 1971 O'Hara's *Collected Poems* won the National Book Award, and he is now widely recognized as one of a number of important poets who came to artistic maturity in the 1950's and 1960's. His work is represented in most widely-circulated anthologies of contemporary American poetry.[3] Two well known books on postwar poetry—Paul Carroll's *The Poem In Its Skin* and Richard Howard's *Alone With America*—each include an entire chapter on O'Hara's work. These critics and anthologists have placed O'Hara in the company of poets like John Ashbery, John Berryman, Allen Ginsberg, Denise Levertov, Robert Lowell, Sylvia Plath and James Wright. But unlike some of these figures— Plath and Lowell especially—O'Hara has not yet received widespread critical recognition, and his position in American literature is still somewhat problematic.

O'Hara's critics—some of the best of whom have been Paul Carroll, Charles Altieri, Helen Vendler, and Marjorie Perloff— tend to stress O'Hara's originality. In Carroll's early essay on "The Day Lady Died" he writes that what makes it "a poem, it seems to me, is the nerve evident in the very act of writing it.

Think of it as a poem 'about' the excitement of the man writing
as he decides to include all of those 'unpoetic' existential places,
names and events. In short, here is an original 'act' in creating
a poem. Such audacity is exciting."[4] Altieri agrees, and goes on
to examine the philosophical necessity for such newness: "Carroll
is correct in insisting that 'The Day Lady Died' is a crucial
touchstone for contemporary poetry. . . . Not only poetry, but even
some of the basic values of civilized life can be discovered by
pushing further than the past into the manifold particulars and
the textures of domestic contemporary life."[5]

Helen Vendler, in her review of the *Collected Poems,* also
emphasizes the importance of O'Hara's pioneering originality:
"Some of O'Hara's poems are already deservedly famous, for the
best reason in the world: nobody has done anything like them in
English." In O'Hara's unprecedented inclusion of a bewildering
array of domestic detail she also sees his chief weakness, "his
radical incapacity for abstraction . . . and his lack of a com-
fortable form (he veered wildly from long to short, with no
particular reason in many cases for either choice)."[6] Yet she
also acknowledges the overall importance of O'Hara's contri-
bution to American poetry as being founded on this arbitrariness,
this radical avoidance of abstraction. O'Hara, she asserts in
conclusion, "in his fine multiplicity and his utter absence of
what might be called an intellectual syntax, [is] a poet to be
reckoned with, a new species" (20).

Marjorie Perloff, in the preface to her book *Frank O'Hara: Poet
Among Painters,* defines O'Hara's originality as a fusion of a
wide variety of literary and extraliterary influences. She concludes that "The result of assimilating such a variety of influences
is the creation of a new kind of lyric poem." And she avows her
of "growing conviction that O'Hara is one of the central poets
of the postwar period, and that his influence will continue to
grow in years to come."

O'Hara's critics are in general agreement that his importance
is based on true originality, and that he has to be considered
in his own right. But O'Hara is not only new, he is also good
by the most basic (and most important) standard: his poems
are touching and complex. They create an ambiance of feeling
that can only be found in them and nowhere else; they underline
feelings that are now more likely to be recognized because

O'Hara wrote about them. In the final analysis, it is only necessary to read a dozen lines or so of any good O'Hara poem to realize not only the originality of his voice, but also its distinctive expressiveness. Here, for a final example, is some of "Lisztiana," a little love poem (probably written while the poet was listening to the music of Franz Liszt):

> A ribbon is floating in the air,
> spring breeze, yellow, white ribbon,
> tossing and catching on itself,
> panting like a Maltese terrier.
> Now it has discovered the earth's
> warm cleavage and drifts slowly down.
> Are you crying over what we've lost
> by not being near each other, hardly
> at all?
>
>   . . . .
>   And now again
> it is drifting, like a kiss on the air,
> emblem of our losing, while the white
> horses neigh and stomp upon the Arctic.   (242–43)

O'Hara keeps things nicely in motion here (saying "emblem of our *losing*" for example, rather than *loss*) and creates something of the floating effect of music. The final image of the white horses in the Arctic—white on white—is adventurous in a painterly way, full of an almost invisible energy. But the only truly remarkable feature of this poem is the jarring, perhaps absurd, almost comical image of the Maltese terrier burrowing into the earth's "cleavage" like a lap dog into its mistress. Perhaps the "panting" of this terrier leads to the "crying" that comes later and makes it more convincing. Yet for whatever reason it is there, the image of warmth and intimacy leading to one of separation contributes immeasurably to the effect of drenching sadness, almost to the point of ferocity, that this poem, like Liszt's music, evokes.

Yet there is an irritating, even if enlivening, arbitrariness about this image of the Maltese terrier. It is like the "Polish rudder" in "To the Harbormaster," (a beautiful, wistful poem for Larry Rivers). Recently the composer Elizabeth Swados set "To the Harbormaster" to music for her Broadway produc-

tion, *Nightclub Cantata*. Yet she took out the word "Polish"
in the phrase: "I am hard alee with my Polish rudder/ in my
hand...." Indeed, "To the Harbormaster" flowed more peacefully and serenely to its guitar accompaniment without its
"Polish rudder," an impenetrably private reference to Rivers's
Polish background. But when it was taken out, the poem—with
its brave resistance to easy lyricism, with its insistence on the
playful, the arbitrary, the accidental—ceased to be O'Hara's.
O'Hara's little Polish in-joke might be thought of as a hardening
agent to keep the emotional substance of the poem solid. Like the
Maltese terrier in "Lisztiana" it is his signature in the poem, and
no one else could have written it quite that way.

Notes and References

Chapter One

1. *Planet News* (San Francisco: City Lights, 1968), pp. 135–36.
2. In an interview with the author at the Museum of Modern Art, July 20, 1976.
3. *Frank O'Hara: Poet Among Painters* (New York, 1977), pp. 96–105.
4. "Life Among the Stones," *Location* (Spring, 1963), p. 97.
5. "The Virtues of the Alterable," *Parnassus* (Fall/Winter 1972), p. 20.
6. Poems by John Ashbery, Kenneth Koch and James Schuyler cited here can all be found in Padgett and Shapiro's anthology, except for Kenneth Koch's "Permanently" which appeared in *Thank You and Other Poems* (New York: Grove Press, 1962), p. 63.

Chapter Two

1. "The Virtues of the Alterable," *Parnassus* (Fall/Winter 1972), p. 7.
2. "The Story of Frank O'Hara: Of Manhattan, The Son," *Gay* (April 17, 1972), p. 5.
3. "Frank O'Hara's Poetry and the Possibility of a Gay Oppositional Praxis," from the author's typescript.

Chapter Three

1. "Larry Rivers: Why I Paint As I Do," *Horizon* (September–October 1959), pp. 95–102; reprinted in *Art Chronicles*, pp. 106–20. Further citations will be to *AC*.
2. See John Gruen's description of O'Hara's relationship with Berkson in *The Party's Over Now* (New York, 1972), p. 148. Gruen says that "Gossip ran along the usual lines in our crowd—namely, that Frank and Bill Berkson were lovers. In this instance the gossip seems to have been wrong. While Bill was extremely handsome, dressed with exquisite taste, and was a constant companion to the

gifted young homosexuals we all knew, it appears he never went to bed with any of them, including Frank." Yet Berkson may have been something of a tease. Gruen reports that during a visit to Water Mill, Long Island, Berkson and O'Hara were "inseparable on that summer day, giggling, gossiping, and having a splendid time. At one point we watched them doff their bathing trunks and race into the sea, a shocking thing to do at the time" (p. 147).

3. *Frank O'Hara: Poet Among Painters*, p. 174.

Chapter Four

1. These lines are found as quoted in section 37 of the 1855 version of the poem, and slightly changed in subsequent versions. The 1855 version can be found in *The Portable Walt Whitman*, edited by Mark Van Doren (New York: Viking, 1945).

2. Composed a year earlier (in 1955), though in stanzas with shorter lines, this passage is integrated so perfectly into "In Memory of My Feelings" that it may be regarded as the origin of much of the imagery of the poem as a whole. Adding only one item, the "Hittite in love with a horse," to link the passage with the other Arabian images, O'Hara could then make the passage serve as a meeting ground for the motifs that bind the poem together. For the original version of the passage see Allen's note to the poem in *The Collected Poems*, p. 538.

3. Joe LeSueur (the Joe of "Joe's Jacket") recalled this to me in an interview in New York on July 19, 1976.

4. *The Complete Poems of D.H. Lawrence*, edited by Vivian de Sola Pinto and Warren Roberts (New York: Viking, 1971), p. 716.

Chapter Five

1. V. R. Lang, a young poet and playwright, O'Hara's friend from his Cambridge years, died of cancer in 1956 at the age of thirty-two. O'Hara never could, or never chose to write an elegy for her. Yet *The Collected Poems* pays tribute to their close friendship by inadvertently including Lang's poem "To Frank O'Hara's Angel" as one of O'Hara's own.

2. The other elegies for Dean are "To An Actor Who Died," "For James Dean," and "Thinking of James Dean."

3. *Contemporary American Poetry*, ed. A. Poulin, Jr. (Boston: Little, Brown, 1971), p. 390.

4. Kenneth Koch said in a conversation with me that on the night O'Hara is recalling in his elegy Holiday's voice was quite

hoarse. She "whispered" because she was ill and could hardly sing. This suggests that it may have been sympathy, coupled with aesthetic awe, that immobilized O'Hara.

5. See particularly "Beautiful Lofty Things," *The Collected Poems of W.B. Yeats* (New York: Macmillan, 1956), p. 300.

6. I will be referring in this discussion to Roger Shattuck's translation of Apollinaire's poem in *Selected Writings* (New York: New Directions, 1948), pp. 89–91.

7. This sequence includes "Joe's Jacket," "You Are Gorgeous and I'm Coming," "Saint," "Personal Poem," "Variations on Pasternak's 'Mein Liebchen, Was Willst du Noch Mehr?'," "To You,," "Les Luths," "Leafing Through Florida," "Poem (Now the violets are all gone, the rhinoceroses, the cymbals)," "Poem V (F) W," "Poem 'À la recherche d'Gertrude Stein'," "Variations on the 'Tree of Heaven' (In the Janis Gallery)," "Poem (Light clarity avocado salad in the morning)," "Hôtel Transylvanie," "Poem (So many echoes in my head)," "Present," "Poem (That's not a cross look it's a sign of life)," "Sudden Snow," "Avenue A," "Now That I Am in Madrid and Can Think," "Having a Coke with You," "Song (I am stuck in traffic in a taxicab)," "An Airplane Whistle (After Heine)," "Trying to Figure Out What You Feel," "Cohasset," "Poem (Some days I feel that I exude a fine dust)," "Song (Did you see me walking by the Buick Repairs?)," "Ballad," "Flag Day," "Steps," "Those Who Are Dreaming, A Play About St. Paul," "A Warm Day for December," "Variations on Saturday," "What Appears to Be Yours," "You at the Pump," "Cornkind," "[The light comes on by itself]," "To Canada (For Washington's Birthday)," "The Anthology of Lonely Days," "Vincent and I Inaugurate a Movie Theatre," "Vincent," "Vincent (2)," "At Kamin's Dance Bookshop," "Poem (Twin spheres full of fur and noise)," "St. Paul and All That," and "A Chardin in Need of Cleaning."

8. Though Vincent's name (or his middle name, Paul) is mentioned in many of these poems, in many other instances it is by no means explicit who the beloved is. The dating suggests that it is Warren, and in my discussion I use the name "Vincent" to indicate the beloved even when O'Hara does not. But in doing so I am referring to Vincent as one might refer to a character in a work of fiction; I have little knowledge of the actual Vincent Warren. My main concern here is to show that the love poems can be read as a continuous narrative. The question of the true origin of these poems, or their basis in O'Hara's life, is not my primary concern here.

9. "The Virtues of the Alterable," *Parnassus* (Fall/Winter 1972), p. 16.

Chapter Six

1. W[infield] T[ownley] S[cott], "The Everyday and the Fanciful," *Saturday Review* (April 12, 1958), p. 72.

2. *Against Interpretation* (New York: Farrar, Straus and Giroux, 1966), pp. 287–88. Further references to Sontag's essay will be noted in parentheses in the text.

3. *Frank O'Hara: Poet Among Painters*, p. 45. In his title, however, O'Hara is referring to the lonely schoolboy, Samuel Taylor Coleridge, who went on to write *Biographia Literaria*.

4. I will be relying on, and quoting from George Reavy's translation in *The Bedbug and Selected Poetry*, ed. Patrica Blake (Cleveland, Ohio: The World Publishing Co., 1960), pp. 137–43.

5. These lines are taken from John Ashbery's translation, "That Memory," in *The Poetry of Surrealism: An Anthology*, ed. Michael Benedikt (Boston: Little, Brown, 1974), p. 79.

Chapter Seven

1. *Dr. Zhivago*, trans. Max Hayward and Manya Harari (New York: Pantheon, 1958), p. 489. Further references will be noted in the text.

2. Phillip Lopate, *The Daily Round* (New York: Sun, 1976), p. 46.

3. O'Hara's work has been included in Donald Allen's *The New American Poetry, 1945–60* (New York: Grove Press, 1960), John Hollander's *Poems of Our Moment* (New York: Bobbs-Merrill, 1968), Mark Strand's *Contemporary American Poetry* (New York: The World Publishing Co., 1969), Miller Williams's *Contemporary Poetry in America* (New York: Random House, 1973), Al Poulin's *Contemporary American Poetry* (Boston: Houghton Mifflin, 1971), and Richard Ellmann and Robert O'Clair's *The Norton Anthology of Modern Poetry* (New York: W. W. Norton, 1973), among others.

4. *The Poem in Its Skin* (Chicago, 1968), p. 163.

5. "The Significance of Frank O'Hara," *Iowa Review*, 4 (Winter 1973), 104.

6. "The Virtues of the Alterable," *Parnassus: Poetry in Review*, I, 6.

Selected Bibliography

Bibliography

Alex Smith is currently preparing a complete bibliography of Frank O'Hara for Garland Publishing Company.

Primary Sources

1. O'Hara's Poetry

ALLEN, DONALD, ed. *The Collected Poems of Frank O'Hara* (New York: Knopf, 1971), supplemented by:

————. *Early Writing* and *Poems Retrieved* (Bolinas, California: Grey Fox Press, 1977). Contains nearly all the poems of Frank O'Hara that have so far been discovered and comprises the definitive edition. These volumes supersede the following earlier collections, in chronolgical order:

A City Winter. New York: Tibor de Nagy Gallery Editions, 1952.

Oranges. New York: Tibor de Nagy Gallery Editions, 1953.

Meditations in An Emergency. New York: Grove Press, 1957; 2nd ed., 1967.

Second Avenue. New York: Totem Press-Corinth Books, 1960.

Odes. New York: Tiber Press, 1960; rpt. New York: The Poets Press, 1969.

Audit/Poetry issue featuring Frank O'Hara, IV (Spring, 1964).

Lunch Poems. San Francisco: City Lights Books, 1964.

Love Poems (Tentative Title). New York: Tibor de Nagy Gallery Editions, 1965.

In Memory of My Feelings. New York: Museum of Modern Art, 1967. A commemorative volume illustrated by thirty American artists.

A generous selection of O'Hara's poems can also be found in *The Selected Poems of Frank O'Hara* (New York: Knopf, 1974).

165

2. Other Writings by Frank O'Hara

Art Chronicles 1954–66. New York: Braziller, 1975.

Selected Plays. New York: Full Court Press, 1978.

Standing Still and Walking in New York. Bolinas, California: Grey Fox Press, 1975. A collection of essays, art criticism, statements on poetry, and the text of an interview with O'Hara by Edward Lucie-Smith.

O'Hara's unfinished novel, "The 4th of July," and a number of short stories remain unpublished. An edition of O'Hara's letters has yet to be announced.

SECONDARY SOURCES

1. Books about Frank O'Hara

BERKSON, BILL and JOE LESUEUR, eds. *Homage to Frank O'Hara.* Volume 11/12 of *Big Sky*, published in Bolinas, California, Summer 1978. A fascinating and varied composite portrait of O'Hara by his numerous friends (many of whom are well known artists and writers) in the form of a collection of memoirs, critical essays, poems, photographs, and drawings. Also contains the transcripts of two films about O'Hara.

PERLOFF, MARJORIE. *Frank O'Hara: Poet Among Painters.* New York: George Braziller, 1977. A well-informed study emphasizing the development of O'Hara's poetry, its cultural context, and the literary and artistic influences that contributed to it. Much useful biographical information gathered from letters and interviews. Ms. Perloff's "New Thresholds, Old Anatomies: Contemporary Poetry and the Limits of Exegesis," *Iowa Review*, 5 (Winter 1974), 83–99, should also be consulted since it serves as a methodological preface for this book.

2. Articles and chapters of books discussing O'Hara

ALTIERI, CHARLES. "The Significance of Frank O'Hara." *Iowa Review*, 4 (Winter 1973), 90–104. A major article in which O'Hara's "fictive world" is described in philosophical terms and seen as the origin of his poetic strategies.

BERKSON, BILL. "Frank O'Hara and His Poems." *Art and Literature*, 12 (Spring 1967), 50–64. Description of O'Hara's personality, interests, intellectual stance, and poetic voice by a close friend and frequent collaborator.

BYRON, STUART. "The Story of Frank O'Hara: Of Manhattan, The

Son." *Gay* (April 17, 1972), 5. O'Hara seen as a poet of both the pain and the "humorous commonplaces of gay life."

CARROLL, PAUL. "An Impure Poem About July 17, 1959." *The Poem in Its Skin* (Chicago: Big Table, 1968). A pioneering essay on "The Day Lady Died" in which O'Hara's use of details without symbolic intention is explored under the rubric of the "impure" poem.

GRUEN, JOHN. *The Party's Over Now: Reminiscences of the Fifties— New York's Artists, Writers, Musicians, and their Friends* (New York: The Viking Press, 1972). Gruen devotes a chapter to O'Hara, discussing his relationships with friends (particularly Bill Berkson, who is interviewed) and also his activities as a writer of lyrics for musicals composed by Gruen.

HOLAHAN, SUSAN. "Frank O'Hara's Poetry." *American Poetry Since 1960, Some Critical Perspectives*, ed. Robert B. Shaw (Cheadle Hulme, England: Carcanet Press, 1973). An enthusiastic, but impressionistic survey of O'Hara's poetry, focusing briefly on the city as subject and setting, O'Hara's syntax, his "selves," and his possible fear of self-confrontation.

HOLLAND, NORMAN. *Poems in Persons, An Introduction to the Psychoanalysis of Literature* (New York: Norton, 1973), pp. 120–26. A reply to Carroll's essay on "The Day Lady Died." Holland's appreciative and penetrating reading demonstrates that the imagery in O'Hara's poem is psychologically coherent and deserving of analysis, and not merely arbitrary and "impure."

HOWARD, RICHARD. *Alone With America* (New York: Atheneum, 1969), pp. 396–412. This account contains some unfortunate errors and obscurities, but also a valuable discussion of the theme of death in O'Hara's poems and critical writings and its relationship to O'Hara's poetics, his "confidence in chaos." Howard draws attention to poems and passages that have been overlooked or ignored by later critics.

KOCH, KENNETH. "All the Imagination Can Hold." *New Republic*, January 1 and 8, 1972, pp. 23–24. A major review of *The Collected Poems*. Koch (O'Hara's close friend) articulates with brilliance and exactitude the unique pleasures and strengths of O'Hara's verse. Draws important distinction between O'Hara's poetry and its Surrealist influences.

LIBBY, ANTHONY. "O'Hara on the Silver Range." *Contemporary Literature*, 17 (Spring 1976), 140–62. In this excellent essay, painting—that of Rivers, de Kooning, and especially Pollock— serves as an illuminating metaphor for the techniques and effects of O'Hara's poetry.

MOLESWORTH, CHARLES. "'The Clear Architecture of the Nerves': The Poetry of Frank O'Hara." *Iowa Review*, 6 (Summer-Fall 1975), 61–73. Though the sharpest criticisms are reserved for O'Hara's poetic followers, this provocative article resolves its ambivalent hostility and admiration for O'Hara by labeling his improvisatory stance typically "American."

MYERS, JOHN BERNARD. *The Poets of the New York School*, selected and edited by John Bernard Myers (Philadelphia: Falcon Press, 1969). O'Hara's first publisher refers to him in the introduction to this anthology as one of a "coterie" of writers turning to the plastic arts for cultural nourishment and deriving their lineage from French Surrealism. Describes the origin of this group and O'Hara's central position in it.

RIVERS, LARRY. "Life Among the Stones." *Location*, Spring 1963, pp. 90–98. An account of the Rivers-O'Hara collaboration on *Stones*, a series of lithographed poem-drawings.

SCHUYLER, JAMES. "Frank O'Hara: Poet Among Painters." *Art News* 73 (May 1974), 44–45. Review of the Whitney Museum's show commemorating O'Hara and brief memoir of O'Hara as poet, curator, and person. Schuyler, O'Hara's longtime friend, recounts the circumstances under which some of the poems were written.

SHAPIRO, DAVID. "Frank O'Hara." *Contemporary Poets*, ed. James Vinson, 2nd ed. (New York: St. Martin's Press, 1975), pp. 1778–81. Brief but suggestive survey of O'Hara's work by a gifted younger poet.

VENDLER, HELEN. "The Virtues of the Alterable." *Parnassus: Poetry in Review*, 1 (Fall/Winter 1972), 5–20. A major review of O'Hara's *Collected Poems*. Cites some of O'Hara's key aesthetic pleasures, as well as his failings.

Index